# A Practical Guide to Teaching Reading in the Early Years

Ann Browne

P·C·P
Paul Chapman
Publishing Ltd

First published 1998

 Paul Chapman Publishing Ltd
A SAGE Publications Company
6 Bonhill Street
London EC2A 4PU

SAGE Publications Inc.
2455 Teller Road
Thousand Oaks, California 91320

SAGE Publications India Pvt Ltd
32, M-Block Market
Greater Kailash-I
New Delhi 110 048

**British Cataloguing in Publication Data**

A catalogue record for this book is available from the British Library

    ISBN 1 85396 416 6
    ISBN 1 85396 400 X (pbk)

**Library of Congress catalog card number available**

Typeset by Dorwyn Ltd, Rowlands Castle, Hampshire
Printed and bound in Great Britain by Athenaeum Press, Tyne & Wear

A B C D E F 3 2 1 0 9 8

# Contents

# Introduction

Knowing about reading, planning a reading curriculum and managing a class so there is sufficient time to teach every child to read often seem to be insurmountable problems at the start of a teaching career. Even after many years of experience teachers can still lack confidence in their ability to teach reading effectively. There is no shortage of advice from statutory bodies, researchers, lecturers, teachers, parents and the media. The very multitude of the advice available is in itself confusing since it is often conflicting. What is the place of phonics in learning to read? What does a real books approach mean? What does research have to offer the teacher? How do I teach children to read well?

Every day adults and children read a huge variety of texts which demand the use of many different strategies. Reading is a flexible activity which involves the use of a variety of cognitive skills. It is not a simple activity and consequently there are no simple solutions to the question of how to teach reading. It requires knowledgeable practitioners who appreciate its complexity and are willing to take a flexible approach to teaching if it is to be taught well.

It is probably still true that 'there is no one method, medium, approach, device or philosophy that holds the key to the process of learning to read' (DES, 1975, para. b, p.77). Experience and research have shown that teachers who create environments in which learning can occur easily are more successful than those who adhere to particular methods or materials. Teachers who are aware of the complexity of the activity, clear about teaching aims and intentions and who plan for reading so that all aspects are covered regularly in a purposeful and structured way will help children to learn to read and to appreciate the place of reading in their lives.

The authors of the Bullock Report (*ibid.*, para. 6.2, p. 77) went on to write: 'We believe that the knowledge does exist to improve the teaching of reading, but that it does not lie in the triumphant discovery or re-discovery, of a particular formula.' I share their belief and with this sentence in mind I have written this book to try to lead readers through what can at times seem a confusing and difficult area. My intention has been to clarify some of the jargon and anecdotal practices that are associated with reading and to present some suggestions about the teaching of reading in the early years. I have taken as the starting point the advice which HMI have consistently offered in their reports on reading since the early 1990s and which is now enshrined in the National Curriculum for Initial Teacher Training (TTA, 1997) and the National Literacy Strategy (DfEE, 1997). In these documents it is suggested that those who teach reading well have a thorough knowledge of the subject and are effective classroom managers.

We are entering a period of immense curriculum change in literacy. Teachers are being asked to adopt unfamiliar approaches to teaching reading and students are entering classrooms where these new practices are not yet established. This book is intended to help those who work with young children, from nursery to the beginning of Key Stage 2, to implement the new requirements for reading. It examines the statutory requirements, classroom management techniques, assessment and approaches to planning for reading and places these practical considerations in the context of up-to-date thinking about learning to read. The first chapters of the book are intended to provide readers with information about reading. They introduce readers to the knowledge and understanding that need to underpin good teaching. Later chapters look at effective classroom organisation and suggest ways of managing the reading curriculum in the early years. These two aspects, subject knowledge and pedagogy, are drawn together in the final chapter which is concerned with planning.

Reading can be one of the most rewarding, satisfying and useful human activities. I hope that this book encourages readers, who may be student teachers or experienced practitioners, to explore the challenges and complexities of teaching reading and to convey its possibilities to the young children they teach.

*Ann Browne*
*April 1998*

# 1

# Understanding reading

## Introduction

Despite all the research that has been undertaken into reading skills, reading development, reading methods, reading habits, reading standards and the uses of literacy, there is still no single description of the reading process or one agreed way of helping children to become readers. Understanding reading is not a simple matter. However, in order to teach effectively, teachers need to know as much as possible about what they are teaching and why, and to be aware of some of the issues that are frequently raised about reading.

The personal definition we have of reading, the purposes for reading we identify, how we ourselves use reading and how we think it is and should be used by others all influence why we consider literacy to be important. Teachers have professional knowledge about how children learn, the skills children need in order to become readers and the conditions which best support learning and learning to read. When they are teaching, they combine their personal understanding and their professional expertise. Both affect the way in which the reading curriculum is realised and perceived by pupils in school.

Cairney (1994, p. 12) has suggested that teachers' personal understanding of literacy can have a significant impact on pupils: 'when teachers impose limited definitions of what it is to be literate on their students, many inappropriate demonstrations of literacy are offered. This in turn can lead to similarly inappropriate literacy practices.' Conversely, informed and broad definitions which are based on knowledge and understanding may be the foundation for appropriate expectations and practices.

The intention of this chapter is to help readers to begin to appreciate the complexity of reading, to consider how their own perceptions of reading might affect their teaching and to consider what constitutes a broad, balanced and appropriate reading curriculum for young children.

# What reading is for

There is a general assumption that being able to read is a good thing. No one is likely to dispute this but, rather than taking the importance of literacy for granted, teachers need to be able to articulate why. As professionals who spend a large part of each working day teaching children to read, they need to have thought about why literacy is important and what benefits readers have over non-readers. Having a considered awareness of the broader aspects of teaching and learning is what separates teachers from non-professionals. Many people are able to offer suggestions about reading based on commonsense, personal experience and vested interest but these are limiting ways of thinking about reading, since they tend to rely on anecdotes and particular examples. Teachers need to go beyond the starting point of common sense and develop a deeper appreciation of reading so that they are in a position to teach all children to read whatever their experience. As part of their professional understanding teachers need to have reflected on the many reasons for becoming a reader and the range of ways in which reading can be used as well as knowing how to teach reading. Knowledge and awareness underpin a planned, well organised and effective curriculum and affect what and how children learn about reading.

Up until the middle of the twentieth century the uses of reading for most people were considerably limited by why they were taught to read and the way in which they were taught. The teaching they received was not intended to produce independent readers and writers. At school the majority of children practised the skills that would enable them to become efficient clerical workers. They were expected to be able to read and copy simple passages and occasionally write short texts. The literacy curriculum was not designed to develop people who would question or actively participate in society. It did not anticipate the need for continued learning, changes in circumstances or the critical use of literacy. For the most part, its chief concern was to produce disciplined, obedient workers who could serve the needs of employers.

We now recognise that reading has a great many more purposes than those identified in the past. There is no area of our lives that does not involve reading. There is now a much greater awareness of the contribution reading can make to individual growth and in enabling people to meet the changing demands of a complex society. Individuals need to be able to use literacy differently depending on their personality and their needs. The purpose to which literacy is put can vary in different locations and at different times. It can be used differently in the home, school, the wider world and in employment. The way children are taught and the curriculum that is offered to them now need to prepare them for the multiple uses of reading they will encounter in their lives.

Reading can enable individuals to meet personal needs and attain individual goals. It can be a source of fulfilment and pleasure. At a personal level, reading fiction or non-fiction related to interests or leisure pursuits can bring satisfaction and enjoyment. Being able to read critically and analytically extends experience, brings access to diverse ideas, allows the exploration of alternative points of view, and enables individuals to discriminate and make choices. It is a means of acquiring ideas and enables people to reflect on their existing values and those held by others in different circumstances. Engaging with print promotes the ability to think about issues and ideas and develops understanding and agility with language in all its forms. Reading can enrich one's life. It has the potential to liberate individuals from confining circumstances through stimulating their imaginations or providing them with the means to make real changes.

The functional uses of reading in school and in most workplaces continue to be important but in order to fulfil these children need to be able to read flexibly and critically. In school children are required to read books and printed information to support their learning across all areas of the curriculum. They are expected to develop the skill of independent learning using all kinds of texts on a wide range of subjects. Through their use of the written word, children are expected to develop an understanding of the world by finding out about life in other times, places and circumstances and the experiments and inventions that have changed our lives. The literacy demands of the world beyond the primary classroom are constantly increasing. Most, if not all, jobs now require employees to be flexibly literate. Increasingly, workers need to understand a wide range of text types including instructions, directions, maps, addresses, letters and memos and to analyse and respond to written information quickly and accurately.

Official references to literacy often stress its social function and its benefits to society as a whole and say little about the significance of being able to read for individuals. They link illiteracy with poverty, underdevelopment, child health and economic, social and cultural exclusion (UNESCO, 1988). This view is strongly represented in *A Reading Revolution* (Barber, 1997, p. 6) where it is stated that 'Young people who fail in the education system will be all too likely to become part of a group of people living in our society but not of it, unable to act as employees, citizens or even, perhaps, parents' and 'illiteracy is costly not just for the individuals concerned but for the country as a whole . . . Making significant inroads into illiteracy, therefore, not only gives children and young people better prospects but also saves money and enhances overall economic performance' (*ibid.*, p. 1).

The relationship between being able to read and employment and financial independence is often at the root of parents' anxieties about their children's reading development. However there seems to be little historical justification for this view: 'Merely teaching men to read and write does not work miracles; if there are not enough jobs for men able to work, teaching more men to read and write will not create them' (Freire, 1972, p. 25). On its own literacy does not necessarily result in achievement, economic well-being and fulfilment, nor is it a solution for economic and social ills because other factors such as gender, race, location, class, culture and socioeconomic status all affect people's opportunities to capitalise upon what they learn at school. Additionally, if people do not realise what reading can do for them, they may not know how to use their ability to change the circumstances of their lives. When the opportunities for change are available and recognised reading can contribute to enhancement by giving people access to information, and qualifications. It is using literacy rather than having it that is likely to lead to cognitive and personal gains.

Parents, employers, governments and teachers may all define the uses of reading in different ways. Each group has its own particular concerns and will prioritise some of the many different uses of reading depending on their own interests. Parents may consider that it is useful because it will help their children to get well paid and satisfying work. Employers regard literate employees as effective workers. Politicians believe that having a literate population will reduce public spending and contribute to the well-being of society. Teachers, as members of society, may share many of these opinions. They will also have their own personal perspective. They will be very aware of the importance of reading for learning in school and how the ability and achievement of the children they teach are often measured by and through reading. As professionals who are often judged by the standards their pupils achieve in reading, teachers may also consider that learning to read is important because good results are an indicator of their own success. There is little doubt that schooling, work, leisure and citizenship are increasingly dependent on being able to read a range of material. To be able to use reading in school and in society, for work and functional reasons, is important but these reasons for reading are externally defined, represent a limited and partial view of the benefits of being able to read and are far removed from the interests of young children.

Teachers need to have a complete picture of the uses of reading and to understand why they are expected to prioritise the teaching of reading. They need to be able to appreciate the individual and societal, personal and functional, immediate and future applications of reading. They need to be able to see the benefits of reading from the learner's perspective rather than their own. Each individual reader will have his or her own reasons for reading and will want to use reading for a broad range of purposes. Ideally readers should be able to choose how to use their ability to achieve their own ends, whatever these may be, and it is the teacher's responsibility to provide for that choice. The teacher's role is to ensure that children develop the ability to read in whatever way they choose or need now and in the future. Our aspirations for children's achievements in reading should be far greater than the aims of the reading curriculum in place earlier in this century or those informed by vested but detached interest.

Recognising the many reasons for learning to read illustrates how people need to be able to use reading in different ways depending on the time, the place and the purpose and has implications for what and how children are taught. Children need to be shown how to become thoughtful and flexible readers. They need a broad reading curriculum which shows them how to apply their skills in different ways according to personal and societal need, that demonstrates that reading is not merely an end in itself or a skill to be presented to others but that it is pleasurable, a source of learning and a means of attaining individual goals. As Meek (1993, p. 97) has written, children should have a chance to discover their own reasons for reading and in so doing 'learn that literacy serves their interests as well as their needs'. In order to achieve this teachers need to see beyond producing children who are 'able to read' and aim to produce children who are 'properly literate' (O'Neil, 1977). Being able to read, to recognise words, follow them across the page and superficially register what has been written without understanding what reading makes possible is not enough. Children need to be able to manipulate and analyse what they read and know that reading has the potential to make a significant and enriching contribution to their lives.

## Reading standards

Many recent reports about reading have been written in a way that implies there is a reading crisis and that large numbers of children are failing to learn to read. They suggest that ineffective teachers are responsible for a fall in reading standards. In reality this does not seem to be the case. There is no consistent evidence of a general decline in reading standards. Suggestions of a reading crisis, particularly in the early years, seem to be based more on assumption than evidence. Whilst there are some children who find learning to reading difficult these are not the majority and their numbers are not increasing. In 1995 the SAT results showed that 80% of 7-year-olds were reading at or above the expected level for their age and this figure has risen each year since then. Evidence from OFSTED's school inspections undertaken in 1995–6 (Hertrich, 1997) revealed that poorer reading scores at Key Stage 1 were found in about 10% of schools but that even there standards varied between classes. This means that satisfactory standards of reading were achieved in 90% of schools and more than 90% of classes. At pre-Key Stage 1 standards were even higher. A recent, large-scale survey into reading standards (Hunter-Grundin, 1997) concluded that reading standards have not fallen in the past 18 years. Other evidence that reading standards have not fallen comes from research reported by Greg Brooks at the 1997 United Kingdom Reading Association conference. His study of national and international surveys of reading revealed that reading standards in Britain have remained almost static for 50 years, with 'no notable decline'.

As long ago as 1953 Lewis wrote (p. 48): 'Common opinion is convinced that illiteracy is increasing . . . this conviction could have been recorded at any time during the last 80 years, if not earlier . . . For about a century we have been concerned about the level of literacy, even though, in fact it may have been steadily rising throughout this time.' This comment seems to be as relevant today as it was almost 50 years ago.

Despite the lack of evidence to support suggestions about falling standards, public and political criticism has informed the new guidelines on teaching reading (DfEE, 1998) which have been accompanied by demands for schools to ensure rapid, quantitative, measurable progress. The publicity surrounding this initiative may mislead many teachers into thinking that children can easily fail to learn to read. In this context it is all too easy to construct a curriculum as if all children are potential or actual failures and to divert the debate about how best to prepare readers for the demands of the twenty-first century into an argument about more or less structured approaches to reading in all schools and for all children. Over-reacting to a crisis that may not exist, designing a curriculum based on limited expectations of success and aiming to teach children to read in the shortest possible time are not the best foundations for a reading programme that will help children to become effective, committed and critical readers. Working with a crude curriculum that fragments reading into an inflexible predetermined set of separate skills that have to be acquired quickly and measured regularly may cause us to loose sight of what reading is and what it is for. No one questions the importance of aiming to help all children to become readers but the context, the curriculum, the methods that are used and the reasons they are offered for becoming literate will affect what children learn about reading, the depth of their learning, the ease with which they learn and their future use of their ability. In the present climate, while the public spotlight is focused on reading, it is very important that teachers do not loose sight of why children learn to read and continue to use their own professional knowledge to make judgements about how and what children should be taught about reading.

## The process of reading

Our present understanding of reading has grown from research and the experience of practitioners that has accumulated over at least one hundred years. Until the middle of this century reading was largely seen as a straightforward translation exercise. All that was involved was learning how to match the printed symbols with their oral equivalents. Since the 1960s many researchers and educators have suggested that making oral correspondences with letters and words is only part of reading. Once readers recognise that reading is a language activity, they interact with text by anticipating meaning and interpreting what they read. Their expectations about what they are reading and the coincidence between what they read and what they expect determines how much use they make of oral and written correspondences. Anyone who has attempted to make sense of an unfamiliar language will recognise that simple, exact translation is not enough. Words and sentences have to be actively interpreted in order to be understood. 'Reading is not deciphering' (Ferreiro and Teberosky, 1983) and, as the first National Curriculum definition of reading stated, 'Reading is much more than the decoding of black marks upon a page: it is a quest for meaning and one which requires the reader to be an active participant' (DES, 1989, para. 16.2).

Reading is a subtle and complex process that involves a relationship between the text and the reader. The text contains information that can be understood by readers who use their skills and experience to do far more than translate written words into oral language equivalents as they engage with the text, construct meanings and explore the message. This understanding of reading draws on investigations into reading and language undertaken by psycholinguists such as Goodman (1975) who has demonstrated the range of cognitive processes and skills that are used when reading, and the work of sociolinguists, particularly Halliday (1975) which has shown that the reading is driven by purpose and dependent on context.

## Models of reading

The different ways in which what happens during the act of read[ing] understood have been summarised in a series of models. Each describes and attempts to explain the way the skills and proces[ses] are involved in the act of reading can be given different e[     ]s. They also represent different definitions of reading. The te[    ] of reading is influenced by the conscious or unconscious as[    ]ons teachers have about what is involved in learning to read[.A]lbeit simplistically, these can be matched to the models of r[   ]. The model teachers and schools subscribe to affects which skills and processes they stress and the order in which they are taught. This is linked to the definition of reading teachers have and their understanding of reading strategies and the uses of reading. Considering the three models of reading can help us to appreciate all the processes involved in reading, understand underlying principles and guide our selection of appropriate practices.

### *The bottom-up model*

The bottom-up model of reading derives from research into the perception, storage and retrieval of linguistic information and refers to approaches to reading which emphasise the identification and analysis of units of language on the page. In this model reading is described as a process that begins with the identification of letters or sounds and later involves using higher levels of linguistic knowledge such as word identification and sentence structure. Learning to read involves making progress through a series of hierarchically sequenced skills beginning with the recognition of letters or words in isolation. This model excludes the wider factors of reading such as the experience, expectations and attitudes of the reader. It does not acknowledge that it is often easier to read and remember words, particularly function words, when they are supported by context. Nor does it take account of findings which show that knowledge about sound symbol correspondences develops through reading rather than prior to it. It does not recognise that readers may read with varying degrees of attention and employ more or less word-level skills according to their purpose for reading and their familiarity with the content and type of the material they are reading. The bottom-up model can lead to a very narrow view of literacy since by focusing on the component skills it excludes the part that is played by the reader and the reader's purposes for reading.

## The top-down model

This model stresses the importance of the qualities and the experiences readers bring to reading. It suggests that readers begin to read by drawing on what they know about the structure and meaningfulness of language, the structure of stories and other genres and their knowledge of the world to predict the general meaning and specific words in the text. Their recreation of meaning is confirmed or disproved by the selective sampling of words and letters. Reading skills such as exact letter and word identification are of secondary importance to the reader's experience and understanding of reading as a purposeful act of communication through language. Phonic and word matching skills which enable the reader to translate letters and words into oral equivalents develop in context and are needed to refine the reader's ability; they are not regarded as the basis of it.

## The interactive model

This model puts the bottom-up and top-down models alongside each other and so includes code features and the broader aspects of reading (Stanovich, 1980). In this model readers are seen as approaching texts with the expectation that they are meaningful. They use their familiarity with the subject-matter, their previous experience of written material, their knowledge about reading and their expectation of meaning to make predictions about content and words. Simultaneously readers use their knowledge about letters, sounds, words and syntax, the cues which arise upwards from the page. These two elements, the reader's knowledge and the textual details, work together. The information gained from word or sound cues shapes the reader's expectations about the meaning, and the anticipation of meaning influences the reader's recognition of the words and the letters the text contains. Continued experience of written texts leads to the automatic recognition of many words and this enables the reader to pay more attention to meaning. In interactive models the reader's understanding of reading as a communicative activity and the skills of reading are both important.

## Teaching approaches

Each of the three models is associated with different approaches to the teaching of reading. The bottom-up model prioritises the early teaching of phonics and the acquisition of a sight vocabulary. Understanding what is read is viewed as a separate skill that develops after

decoding. The top-down model places emphasis on meaningful encounters with print which encourage children to apply their growing
knowledge about communication and their appreciation of language
rules to texts. Readers are placed in situations where they approach
texts with the expectation that they will understand them. The interactive model draws both approaches together so that the reading
programme contains opportunities for children to behave like experienced readers, to apply their existing oral language strategies to written texts and to acquire decoding skills in meaningful contexts. In this
model learning to read involves learning and using developing strategies and newly acquired skills in an integrated way.

When learning to read is regarded either as acquiring a set of skills
or learning to apply existing knowledge, children are deprived of the
help offered by the whole range of strategies available to readers.
Teaching children skills without giving them the information about
their role as readers and why the process is important may result in
the acquisition of knowledge that is not applied. Similarly emphasising the process without providing access to the skills may also be
disabling since it limits children's efforts to recognise what has been
written. When children are presented with meaningful, supported
encounters with print that demonstrate the processes and purposes of
reading and are taught the skills that they require to make reading
easier when they need them, they are being given access to a wide
range of strategies and techniques that should help them to become
successful readers.

Teaching that is based on the interactive model is characterised by
planned opportunities which enable children to

- understand the larger purposes of learning to read;
- understand how reading works;
- become familiar with the content and structure of texts before being
  expected to read alone; and
- receive information about specific strategies in context and when
  they are needed.

## The statutory requirements for reading

The model of teaching reading described in the National Curriculum
(DfE, 1995) closely resembles the interactive approach and supports a
holistic reading programme. It emphasises the need to develop children's awareness of the functions of reading, to immerse them in
print, build on their existing language capabilities and to teach phonic
and word recognition skills alongside wider strategies:

Pupils should be taught to read with fluency, accuracy, under-standing and enjoyment, building on what they already know. In order to help them develop understanding of the nature and pur-pose of reading, they should be given an extensive introduction to books, stories and words in print around them. Pupils should be taught the alphabet, and be made aware of the sounds of spoken language in order to develop phonological awareness. They should also be taught to use various approaches to word identi-fication and recognition, and to use their understanding of gram-matical structure and the meaning of the text as a whole to make sense of print.

(*Ibid.*, p. 6)

Although the National Curriculum orders for reading have influenced the advice about reading contained in the *Desirable Outcomes for Children's Learning* (SCAA, 1996a) it is easy to interpret the description in this document as signalling a skills rather than an interactive approach to reading. The language and literacy programme to be offered to 4-year-olds seems to prioritise letter and word recognition although it does also mention the importance of children enjoying and becoming familiar with books. The suggestions about baseline assessment (SCAA, 1997a) which identify sound, letter and word recognition as appropriate items for assessing reading at the age of 5 again draw attention to reading skills.

The model of reading presented in the *Framework for Teaching* (DfEE, 1998) is intended to match exactly that in the National Curriculum programmes of study. It identifies context, grammatical knowledge, word recognition, graphic information and phonic awareness as the range of cues that readers need to develop and it describes reading as an active process that involves problem-solving, prediction and the use of prior knowledge and experience. Unfortunately the model of teaching that is presented in the *Framework for Teaching* diverts atten-tion away from the interactive approach. The suggestions for planning and teaching the literacy curriculum it contains have grown out of the current anxiety about reading attainment. They are based on the assumption that, at present, children are not learning to read well enough and teachers are not teaching reading effectively. As the inten-tion of the *Framework for Teaching* is to address these shortcomings the document is presented in way that makes reading and the teaching of reading appear very straightforward and achievable in a very short time. It prescribes how work needs to take place at word, sentence and text level and particular attention is given to how and in what order phonics and sight words should be taught and learned. Although teaching at word, sentence and text level is expected to proceed together, word-level work is explained in detail and it seems to be given priority over sentence and text-level strategies.

It is easy to interpret the content of both the *Desirable Outcomes for Children's Learning* (SCAA, 1996a) and the *Framework for Teaching* (DfEE, 1998) as promoting a bottom-up or skills-based model of reading. Both documents are attempting to describe what needs to be learned and how it can be taught in a fairly unsophisticated way. They deliberately present a simplified picture of reading in order to convince teachers and other practitioners that learning to read is simple and teaching reading is straightforward. However there are dangers associated with oversimplification. In order to be easily understood, undeveloped models may only portray one part of the process and do not necessarily show the way in which skills and understanding work together. It is easier to describe how to teach skills than to explain reader behaviour, attitudes and purposes for reading. This can result in advice that seems to emphasise skills and minimise other aspects of reading. Beginning with standards puts enormous pressure on children to get it right very quickly and encourages the fragmentation of reading into easily tested skills. As they are intended as practical documents, neither the *Desirable Outcomes for Children's Learning* (SCAA, 1996a) nor the *Framework for Teaching* (DfEE, 1998) contain a rationale for the aims for reading they outline or discuss what reading can really be for. In particular, the latter has been designed to fulfil the government's aims of economic and social improvement and so an exploration of current thinking about reading and the individual benefits that reading brings may be of less significance to the authors than functional literacy and the speedy acquisition of skills. However knowledge about reading and the personal benefits of being able to read are still important to learners and teachers. They are the background understanding that teachers need in order to provide pupils with a rich and rewarding curriculum.

Interpreting the recommendations contained in these recent documents for the early years superficially may lead to an impoverished and mechanistic reading curriculum. Whilst this may not be the intention, the most recent official advice could result in narrow ways of teaching which give children 'limited instruction in skills for literacy' (Whitehead, 1996, p. 71) and lead to a replication of the reading curriculum provided in the earlier part of this century. Children could be given inappropriate activities which place the emphasis on aspects of reading that are easy to teach and measure, such as knowing sound symbol correspondences and recognising a prescribed set of words. They may be expected to spend large amounts of time on practising and learning basic skills quickly and opportunities to enjoy and investigate reading in meaningful contexts could be marginalised. This is not what HMI (1996) see as desirable. They want children to be exposed to a broad range of texts, to discuss, question, evaluate and respond in depth to what they read, acquire positive attitudes towards books and become readers who enjoy and use books and written material throughout their lives.

Prescribed curricula cannot tell us how to, nor will they necessarily, produce readers who recognise that reading is an important and rewarding pursuit. Children can be taught a set of skills but they cannot be trained to like or use their skills when they are in a position to exercise choice. Being able to recognise words and apply phonic skills is not enough to become a reader. Reading does involve decoding print but it is also an activity that requires interpretation, evaluation and understanding. Using reading involves understanding what reading can do and being disposed to read. In order to be successful and to continue developing as readers children need to acquire skills, knowledge, understanding and identify reading as purposeful and pleasurable. Children's views about worthwhile activities are shaped by the examples they come into contact with. How teachers model the uses of reading, what they recommend, demonstrate, emphasise and cherish has a large effect on how and what pupils learn and on their motivation in the short and long term.

Statutory requirements have an impact on decisions that are made about teaching but they do not prescribe exactly how teachers should work or the activities that teachers plan. They provide a reference point for teaching which require careful reading and thoughtful interpretation so that their content and intentions are implemented through an interactive approach and rich curriculum provision. Teachers can use their own knowledge about reading to add depth to the guidelines when translating advice into practice. Their professional knowledge allows them to create positive contexts for learning. They can decide to teach reading so that children learn the required skills through purposeful encounters with texts. They can take account of the need to show children the purpose and application of reading, introduce them to a range of strategies and ensure that children learn about the wider dimensions of reading. Working in this way capitalises on the developments that have taken place in understanding reading and the reading process. A curriculum that is informed by research, experience and knowledge in addition to the statutory requirements is more likely to be relevant to the needs of young learners. It is more likely to produce thoughtful and committed readers who gain personal satisfaction from reading and who can use their ability to respond to the reading demands of the twenty-first century.

## Young readers

By the time they are 4 most children have learned to use and understand language and have established the foundations for learning to read and write. They have a large oral vocabulary, know about word order and word agreement and are aware that language is for communication. Through their experience as oral language learners, children have already covered some of the preparatory work needed for learning to read. Most young children will also have a considerable awareness of the significance of literacy for coping with everyday life. There is a great deal of evidence that shows young children notice print, ask questions about it, attempt to create it themselves and try to discover what it can do for them (Bissex, 1980; Ferreiro and Teberosky, 1983). Even if there are differences in their direct experience of books, book ownership, discussions about print with others or library membership the majority of children will have some appreciation of written language and what reading is for. They may have experience of story and rhyme, and have seen and participated in literacy events in the home. They may have observed adults paying bills, reading magazines and reading and writing letters and cards. They may know that certain words in their immediate environment such as the names of foodstuffs, shops, streets and toys carry meaning. They may also be able to recognise their own name. All these experiences, gained in meaningful and relevant contexts, will have given even very young children an appreciation of many of the uses of reading.

Whatever the depth of their experience the vast majority of young children have begun to understand that

- print conveys messages that are understood by the reader;
- texts carry information or stories;
- texts can be responded to;
- oral language can be represented by written language;
- there are different sorts of texts;
- reading is a useful and important activity; and
- reading can be enjoyable.

Early years teachers acknowledge that a great deal of literacy learning takes place before or outside school and respect children's early achievements. When they begin to teach children they find out about their experiences, what they know and what they can already do, in order to build on children's existing knowledge and extend their awareness and competence with language in its oral and written forms. This means building on their understanding of reading as well as developing their ability to read. The curriculum they offer will not be inflexible or predetermined but will address and provide for differences in experience and opportunity. It acknowledges that children learn at different rates, in different ways and have different needs. Children's success at learning before school provides clues about the sort of curriculum that will be well matched to the strengths and needs of young learners. A curriculum that pays attention to what young children know about reading and to how they acquired this knowledge will consider reading purposes as well as skills. It will respect the integrity of children and the integrity of the activity. It will recognise that children do not just need to be taught but that they need to be supported as they learn and that they need to learn about the activity as well as learning how to do it. Teaching reading in the early years will take place in positive learning contexts using sensible, multifaceted approaches. It will be undertaken by adults who have explored the process of reading, know why it is important and transmit an infectious enthusiasm for reading. The curriculum which practitioners design will contain genuine opportunities for children to learn about reading in authentic and purposeful ways and enable them to

- behave like readers;
- enjoy books and feel confident about reading;
- read for meaning;
- respond to and interpret texts;
- understand that reading has a role in their lives;
- use reading for their own reasons; and
- become eager and committed readers.

These conditions for learning about literacy can be combined with planned opportunities to develop the word, sentence and text-level key skills readers require. A curriculum that is appropriate to the needs and interests of young children and that is designed by teachers who understand the reading process and have up-to-date information about the teaching of reading is most likely to lead to successful learning and teaching.

Throughout this chapter I have been attempting to show that there is much more to teaching reading than implementing the objectives contained in documents. Any curriculum for reading is located in a context that is defined by the teacher's knowledge and vision of reading and her understanding of young learners. Methodologies and materials require the teacher to interpret and use them in the best possible way. Knowledge about reading and learning enables teachers to make judgements about the curriculum children are offered. Their professional expertise affects the choice and management of activities and, most importantly, the spirit in which reading is offered to children.

## Conclusion

Children's reading abilities develop best when they are given a coherent programme of purposeful activities. The programme needs to
be informed by an understanding of how children learn to read and
why. It needs to take account of the relevance of reading to young
children and how they might need and want to use reading here and
now as well as in the future. It needs to acknowledge the personal,
practical and social benefits of being able to read and aim to produce
readers who develop an enduring love of reading as well as understanding that reading is a useful and practical skill. It needs to build
on what children can already do and should be taught with the expectation of success. Appreciating the complexity of reading, having an
overview of the models of reading and some of the practices that are
associated with them add to our understanding of reading and how to
teach it. The more knowledge that educators have about all aspects of
reading the more they will be able to support developing readers in
flexible and responsive ways and help them to become successfully
literate.

## Further reading

Clay, M. M. (1991) *Becoming Literate: The Construction of Inner Control*,
    Heinemann, Auckland.
Dombey, H. (1992) *Words and Worlds: Reading in the Early Years of School*,
    NATE, Sheffield.
Harrison, C. and Coles, M. (eds) (1992) *The Reading for Real Handbook*,
    Routledge, London.

# 2

# The key skills of reading

---

## Introduction

The key skills of reading are those strategies that help children to read with understanding, fluency, accuracy and enjoyment. In the National Curriculum programme of study for reading (DfE, 1995) they are identified as

- phonic knowledge
- graphic knowledge
- word recognition
- grammatical knowledge
- contextual understanding,

and they correspond to the model of language referred to in the *Framework for Teaching* (DfEE, 1998) where the key skills are represented by three teaching strands at

- word level
- sentence level
- text level.

The overlap between the programme of study and the literacy framework is as follows:

- phonic knowledge – word-level work;
- graphic knowledge – word-level work;
- word recognition – word-level work;
- grammatical knowledge – sentence-level work; and
- contextual understanding – text-level work.

As the reading curriculum that is offered to children is expected to cover all the key skills, this chapter will explore the meaning of these terms and suggest some ways of developing the key skills of reading in the early years.

The National Curriculum (DfE, 1995), the *Framework for Teaching* (DfEE, 1998) and, to a lesser extent, the *Desirable Outcomes for Children's*

*Learning* (SCAA, 1996a) describe the content of the reading curriculum that should be offered to children. However the learning climate and the dispositions that young children need to acquire in order to become successful readers are not described. If children are to make a positive start on becoming life-long readers and literacy learners they need to feel confident in their own abilities and appreciate the rewards that reading brings. Therefore it is vitally important that the key skills are taught and learned in a context where children feel confident about their abilities as readers and acquire and maintain positive attitudes to reading. The chapter begins by exploring the place of attitudes and expectations and suggests ways of developing these effectively.

## Learner dispositions

### *The importance of positive attitudes and confidence*

If teaching is to be successful it is not just the content of the teaching that is provided that is important, learners have to be willing and eager to learn. As experienced learners, we know that as we gain knowledge we develop attitudes towards what we learn and construct a picture of ourselves as learners. Attitudes, self-concept and our perception of the relevance of what we are being taught to our immediate concerns and interests can affect how much and how easily we learn. When most young children start school they have a great deal of optimism about their capacity as learners: they are developing and acquiring skills so rapidly that they naturally assume that what they cannot do today will be possible tomorrow (Hills, 1986). Their confidence and their eagerness to explore the world around them mean that the majority embark on learning to read with enthusiasm. All children need to continue to believe that they will become readers and that learning to read well is normal rather than problematic. Children also need to learn that books are a source of enjoyment and information and to derive pleasure and satisfaction from reading. They need to be convinced of the rewards that learning to read brings. Children who do not learn this lesson early have little reason to invest the energy and attention in learning to read that are needed (Dombey, 1994). Confidence in their ability as readers enables children to take the risks that new learning requires, to make predictions about texts and words, to revise ideas, to correct errors as they read and to ask questions about reading. One of the most important aspects of the teacher's role is to provide a learning context that builds on the attributes most young children bring to school, enabling them to grow in confidence while extending their competence.

Although adults want to develop children's confidence in their ability to learn and their interest in reading they do not always make this clear to children. Some teachers and parents are so concerned about achievement that they transmit their anxieties to children and unconsciously suggest that learning to read is difficult. Children who are acutely aware of the importance of success or who fear failure may approach reading tentatively or competitively. They may be so conscious of adult praise or censure that they become fixed on accuracy and performance and unable to appreciate that reading can be rewarding and books enjoyable. If they do make mistakes or reach a natural plateau in their development they may begin to loose confidence in their ability to read and begin to view reading negatively. This will make it harder for them to learn.

Syvla (1997) has suggested that the types of activities that are provided for children have a strong influence on the attitudes they develop about learning. In her research she found that formal teaching and isolated skill development can lead to disenchantment with learning, low self-esteem and, in the long term, poor performance for many children. When children are expected to learn by acquiring skills in a prescribed order at a particular time any deviation from the programme can be seen as a problem by teachers. Inflexible programmes suggest that learning can only take place in one way. Children who learn in different ways and at a different pace may begin to believe that they are not normal or that they are inferior. These considerations are important when thinking about how the key skills of reading should be developed. Careful choices have to made about how they are taught and the activities and resources that are used in order to avoid alienating young learners.

## *Developing confidence and positive attitudes to reading*

If children are to develop confidence and positive attitudes to reading the following practices need to be avoided:

- learning which places too many abstract demands on young children;
- developing skills in isolation from the context in which they are to be applied;
- repetitive drilling;
- activities that demand right answers;
- emphasising extrinsic rewards;
- a learner deficiency model where children are seen as likely to fail;
- making learning hard;

- obscuring the purposes of learning to read; and
- unnecessary testing.

Instead children need to be presented with opportunities to

- believe in their abilities as developing readers;
- discover that reading is a communicative activity;
- learn in a non-competitive, supportive environment;
- read in a range of situations;
- take control of their own learning by choosing their own books;
- discuss books;
- hear adults share their love of reading in genuine ways;
- make connections between their own experiences and those in books;
- see and hear models of adult readers who engage in and talk about their own reading;
- read complete texts;
- understand that reading is a meaningful activity;
- become familiar with a range of texts and discover favourite texts and authors; and
- have learning experiences that are pitched at the right level.

It is just as important to make it possible for children to learn to read and enthuse them with a love for reading as it is to teach them how to read.

## Understanding the key skills

The interactive model of reading, which was used to inform the National Curriculum programme of study and has been referred to earlier in this book, shows how readers have to combine different kinds of personal and linguistic knowledge with the information that a written text contains in order to read. The knowledge children have to acquire to become confident readers has been identified as the key skills in the official documentation. In the National Curriculum (DfE, 1995) and the *Framework for Teaching* (DfEE, 1998) these skills include grammatical knowledge and contextual understanding which make use of the reader's oral language skills, existing knowledge of the subject-matter expressed in the text, prior experience of books and awareness of how reading works. The three word-level key skills are phonics and graphics and word recognition and refer to the reader's ability to use knowledge of letters, sounds and words. In addition I have included a sixth key skill, bibliographic knowledge, which is the underlying knowledge about books and reading readers need to have.

This is a crucial foundation for reading and is particularly important for very young children. Each key skill plays a part in reading by reducing the number of possible words that have to be consciously recognised during the act of reading because they help readers to identify familiar words quickly and make successful predictions of unknown words. The contribution of each individual key skill is enhanced when it is used in conjunction with the others. All children, at every stage of development, need to learn how to use the full range of strategies the key skills provide flexibly and appropriately in order to be successful at reading, so they all need to be developed throughout the early years.

## Word-level key skills

These include phonic and graphic knowledge and the ability to recognise words on sight. Overemphasising word-level skills may result in a code-cracking approach to reading which prioritises accuracy. When the teaching of reading focuses on correctness and translation children may fail to learn that understanding what is read is important. Placing too much emphasis on word-level skills can interfere with risk-taking strategies such as prediction and self-correction and can obscure the enjoyment of reading and children's appreciation of its relevance to their lives.

### *Understanding phonic knowledge*

Knowing about phonics means understanding the sound system of the English language and appreciating the relationship between sounds and print symbols. In line with recent research into the role of phonic understanding and how children learn about the alphabetic qualities of the language, the National Curriculum (DfE, 1995) and the *Desirable Outcomes for Children's Learning* (SCAA, 1996a) suggest that there are many elements in this key skill and that, contrary to historical and public opinion, it is not appropriate to start with the smallest units of language such as individual letter sounds.

For many years applying phonic knowledge to reading was understood as learning to match letter symbols with their equivalent sounds and translating combined letter sounds into the approximation of a word. Viewing phonics in this way caused many educators to question the value and place of phonic teaching in a reading programme for young children. Simply matching graphemes to phonemes in English is not straightforward because the 26 letters of the alphabet have to represent approximately 44 sounds. This means that some letters can be sounded in a number of ways. For example the *a* in '*all*', '*have*' and '*cake*' is pronounced differently in each word. Other words, many of which young children will meet in their early encounters with print, seem to defy phonic analysis. For example sounding out the individual letters contained in *there* or *was* is unlikely to help children to produce recognisable oral equivalents of these words. As if this were not difficult enough, the individual sounds that are produced when sounding out a word are often distorted by the addition of a neutral vowel as in *c(uh)* rather than *c*. This can make it hard to recognise the oral version of the word that has been spelled out. Introducing children to phonic rules can also be unsafe. Clymer (1963) analysed the generalisability of 45 phonic rules in 2,600 words taken from a number of early reading scheme books. He found that the magic *e* explanation, 'when words end with silent *e*, the preceding *a* or *i* is long', was untrue for 40% of the words he examined.

The act of applying phonic knowledge, even in straightforward cases, involves a number of complex cognitive operations. This again can cause problems for young readers. First, children need to remember the relationship between the 26 letter shapes of the lower-case alphabet and the 44 sounds. Next, to apply this knowledge when reading, they have to segment words into their component parts, then determine the corresponding sounds and finally blend these together to produce a recognisable pronunciation for the words they are reading. Research has shown that children under the age of 6 find it very difficult to segment words into all their constituent phonemes (Goswami, 1994) and that learning and using sound symbol correspondences to decode unfamiliar words are easier after children have had experience of reading texts and recognising whole words (Frith, 1980). Unless children understand that words contain sequences of separable sounds they cannot take the next step of matching the letters in words to individual phonemes.

The work of Goswami and Bryant (1990) has shown that there are sound units other than the phoneme that can be used effectively by young readers. They found that there is a strong connection between children's ability to detect and manipulate the sounds that make up spoken words and their reading development but that this is different from the simple application of individual sound to letter correspondences. They have suggested that in the early stages it is sensitivity to rhyme and the awareness of the units of sound that begin and end words that are related to success at learning to read rather than the knowledge of individual phonemes. These sound units have been termed onset and rime. In a word such as *cat*, the onset is *c* and the rime *at*. In the word *stop* the onset corresponds to *st* and the rime to *op*. Words of two syllables or more may contain two onsets and two rimes. For example in the word *plastic* the onsets are *pl* and *t* and the rhymes *as* and *ic*. Children who are aware of onset and rime have begun to realise that language contains units of sounds that are smaller than the word. Their appreciation that many end units or rimes can be heard in other words helps children to make relationships between words and to analyse similarities and differences in words. For example, *cat* and *hat* share the same rime but have different onsets. Goswami (1994) found that children have little difficulty in discerning onsets and rimes. Perhaps it is because they correspond closely with speech units that they are far more comprehensible to children than individual phonemes.

Once children appreciate onsets and rimes they can be shown how these are linked to the symbols that represent them. Demonstrating this to children can take place when teachers and children say and read nursery rhymes or when the teacher shares stories with rhyming texts with the class. Further examples of words that sound similar can be used to show children that rimes can be heard and seen in many different words. Once they know the sound and the way that it is represented in one word they can be shown how to recognise the rime and the symbols in other words. Goswami (*ibid*.) describes this as making analogies. An analogy in reading involves using the spelling pattern of a word that is known as a basis for reading a new word that contains a similar set of symbols or spelling pattern.

The desirable learning outcomes and programme of study for Key Stage 1 reflect current research into the place of phonics in learning to read. The definition of phonic teaching they give is broad and teachers are asked to provide opportunities for children to recognise sound patterns, rhymes, alliteration and syllables and to identify initial and final sounds in words before learning individual letter sounds and beginning to match these with written symbols. The emphasis is on developing phonological awareness first.

Once children have acquired phonological awareness of syllables, onsets and rimes and are able to make analogies they will be in a better position to learn about phoneme–grapheme relationships and how to analyse words and then synthesise sounds in order to read unknown words. This is because they will have begun to appreciate how spoken language is related to written language and through their experience with onsets and rimes have begun to develop an awareness of phonemes and the alphabetic system of English. By this time they will also have gained some experience of reading and recognising whole words and have a growing understanding of the variability

of the relationship between sounds and symbols in the English language. This should mean that children will be able to make more
effective use of the phonic teaching concerned with individual letters
and sounds. Less technically, but very importantly, they may have
had the opportunity to learn about reading, its pleasures and its purposes, without being distracted or pressured by abstract concepts and
an insistence on accuracy.

If, in addition to learning about the phonological relationship between oral and written language, children have learned that written
language is organised and carries messages in a similar way to speech
before being introduced to phoneme–grapheme relationships, they
will be able to apply their phonic knowledge in combination with
other reading cues. It is when phonics is used in conjunction with
grammatical knowledge and contextual understanding that it works
most efficiently. For example, if in the sentence 'She rode her . . . , the
reader recognises the initial letter of the unknown word as *b* he or she
might insert any word into the sentence that begins with *b*. These
could include words such as *brown*, *bucket*, or *because*, none of which
are appropriate. However if the reader is aware that the unknown
word is a noun (grammatical knowledge), that it is something that can
be ridden (contextual understanding) and that it begins with *b* (phonic
knowledge) he or she is in a far better position to make an informed
guess and produce the word *bike*.

When children have acquired sufficient phonological awareness to
enable them to 'associate sounds with patterns in rhymes, with syllables and with words and letters' (SCAA, 1996, p. 3) and have begun
to make some connections between sounds and written symbols (DfE,
1995; SCAA, 1996a), teachers can begin to provide children with a
more detailed knowledge of phonics in line with the statutory requirements. Adams (1990) suggests that children need to proceed through
the following stages to become competent at using simple phonic
strategies:

- become aware of syllables in words;
- become aware of the different sounds in words;
- split words and syllables into onsets and rimes;
- detect all the sounds in a word and segment words into sounds; and
- change sounds in words, for example *dog* to *dig* or *dig* to *wig*.

Once children are able to manipulate regular phoneme–grapheme relationships they need to be introduced to combinations of letters and
their sounds and spelling patterns. HMI (1996) found that in many
schools phonics teaching did not go beyond the teaching of initial
letter sounds and were critical of this. As the programme of study for

reading and the framework for teaching suggest, the following, increasingly difficult, aspects should be introduced and systematically taught during Key Stage 1:

- initial and final sounds in words;
- short vowel sounds in simple words;
- initial and final consonant blends;
- digraphs where consonants are combined to create new sounds;
- vowel phonemes;
- letter combinations, such as *ear*;
- inconsistencies in phonic patterns, for example *wood* and *food*; and
- the way in which some letters influence the sound of others, for example the vowels in *cake*.

## *Developing phonic knowledge*

- Teach phonological awareness through drawing on children's delight in the rhyme, rhythm and pattern of oral language in meaningful contexts such as exploring language play in jokes, nursery rhymes, poetry, riddles, tongue twisters and songs.
- Relate early phonological awareness to familiar and enjoyable rhyming texts.
- Play games that help children to become familiar with the sounds of language, such as 'I Spy', 'Odd One Out', 'I Went to Market and I Bought a . . .', 'I Packed my Suitcase with a . . .'.
- Encourage experimentation with spelling as this provides insights into the relationship between the sounds and symbols of written language and fosters understanding of words as sequences of sounds that can be matched to sequences of letters.
- Use clapping rhythms to help children to become aware of syllables in words.
- Provide plenty of opportunities for children to hear print brought to life by a familiar voice to develop their awareness of the relationship between written language and the sound system.
- Make time for children simultaneously to listen to and read taped stories so that they can see and hear words together.
- Make personal letter books such as *Calum's C Book* based on the *Berenstain's B Book*.
- Read and use alphabet books with children.
- Use shared reading, group reading and individual reading sessions to make the connection between oral and written language.
- Use enlarged texts for reading poems and rhymes and draw attention to the letters which match the rhyming sounds in words.

- Develop awareness of the sounds of the language through playing language games, singing rhymes and songs and sharing poems.
- Encourage children to use initial sounds to predict unknown words.
- Identify each syllable in multisyllabic words and ask children to pronounce each one and then read the word.
- Make up different versions of traditional rhymes, such as 'Humpty Dumpty sat on his bed, Humpty Dumpty had hurt his head'.
- Ask children to identify letters and groups of letters in words, to match these to sounds and then to pronounce the whole word.
- Use the titles of familiar books to teach children about initial letter sounds and matching graphemes.
- Teach phonics in context so that children can apply their knowledge to reading.
- Revise and return to phonic patterns that have been introduced to ensure learning.
- Collect objects and pictures of words which rhyme and make a rhyme display.
- Establish a 'sound of the week' table to which children contribute items and labels. Use the collection for sorting activities, when some items which begin with a different sound can be included.
- Compose songs that are based on books that have been read in shared reading sessions and incorporate repeated refrains or phrases.
- Do not merely rely on phonic teaching programmes, be resourceful and creative in the choice of activities.

## *Understanding graphic knowledge*

Graphic knowledge is understanding that letters and patterns of letters and the visual details of words provide information that allows words to be recognised by readers. Phonic and graphic strategies are frequently linked since applying phonic knowledge to reading depends on relating sounds to written symbols in order to turn print into oral language. The programme of study for reading links phonics and graphics in the section on phonic knowledge but includes a separate section on graphic knowledge. This acknowledges that graphic information can be used without being translated into its phonic equivalent. Because the first point of contact with print is through the eyes the visual aspects of print are vital.

Young readers often recognise the first letter of words and use this information to produce words that begin in visually similar ways when they encounter unfamiliar words. When they do this they are using graphic knowledge to inform their guesses. They may also use graphic information such as the length and shape of a word to help them remember words that are important or that they see frequently. More precise graphic information can help readers to distinguish between words that are similar. For example by looking at the graphic detail in a word the reader may be able to see the difference between words such as *where* and *when*. Paying attention to spelling patterns in words can enable readers to apply their knowledge about known letter strings such as *ing* or *ight* to unknown words. Recognising known words within unknown words may also help readers to read unfamiliar words. This applies particularly to root words or singular versions of words. For example recognising the root *help*, within the word *helping*, may help a young reader to decipher this longer and possibly newly encountered word. As children become aware of the links between words and of the groups of letters that are often added to words such as prefixes, suffixes, verb endings and plurals they will be developing their graphic strategies that enable them to read a widening vocabulary of words quickly. Graphic knowledge also contributes to understanding since punctuation is also represented graphically and these marks provide readers with important information about the meaning and structure of texts.

## *Developing graphic knowledge*

- Model and encourage close attention to visual aspects of books by reading the pictures in books.
- Read and discuss wordless picture books with children.
- Share caption books and tell children 'this word says . . .'.
- Provide books with detailed illustrations, such as the *Where's Wally?* series.
- Organise print observation walks around the school or the immediate environment.
- Involve children in making displays and draw attention to what is included.
- Play 'I Spy' games.
- Play word games that involve sorting and matching words.
- Discuss words with children.
- Make collections of environmental print which children can cut up, copy, compare and sort.
- Select a word for the week and compile, with the class, a list of words which look similar, begin with the same letter or end with the same letter string.
- Make and display collections of words containing similar spelling patterns, prefixes, suffixes and roots.

- Let children make their names and other words using Play Doh and plastic letters.
- Make a tile alphabet out of clay squares.
- Ask children to look for analogous spelling patterns, words beginning with the same letter or containing the same letter string, and to write these on to charts that can be displayed.
- Discuss and compare words in order to discover similarities and differences.
- Ask children to focus on the ending of a word and to relate the unknown words to known words.
- Take the opportunity provided by shared reading sessions to draw attention to visual features in words and to discuss words.
- Make alphabet books, friezes and posters using familiar words and personal names.
- Reinforce visual awareness of letter patterns and words through providing correct spelling models beneath children's writing and comparing and analysing both children's and adults' versions.
- Include shared writing and scribing as part of the literacy curriculum and discuss aspects of print and words while writing with children.
- Construct morphemic word webs to raise awareness of word structure, spelling patterns and relationships between words. Begin with a word that is familiar to the children and brainstorm other linked words. This can be added to over the course of a week.
- Introduce children to the use of dictionaries to look for correct spellings of words.

## Understanding word recognition

Being able to recognise written words automatically is very helpful when reading since the swift identification of words leaves the reader free to concentrate on the meaning of the text. The look and say method of learning to read (Schonell, 1945) involved children in learning sets of words before reading them in books. In order to memorise the words the children engaged in repetitive activities such as flashcard work, where the teacher held up words for the children to say, and copying and tracing words on worksheets. Not only do these practices obscure the purpose and pleasure of learning to read but they also place a huge burden on young children's memories and do not provide them with any strategies that will enable them to read unknown words. They also emphasise accuracy and performance as the words have to be identified correctly.

The most useful words to be able to recognise on sight are those that are frequently encountered in text, difficult to predict from the context and phonically irregular. In the early years many of these are likely to be function words such as *this*, *the* and *there*. All books contain a high percentage of function words many of which are repeated within the same book and in other books. McNally and Murray (1968) found that

> a, and, he, I, in, is, it, of, that, the, to, was, all, as, at, be, but, are, for, had, have, him, his, not, on, one, said, so, they, we, with, you

comprise more than 25% of the words that young children meet and more recent studies do not conflict with their findings. As these words occur so frequently, children are likely to encounter them regularly as they read books and look at print. Reading a variety of books with others and alone should provide children with sufficient practice to begin to establish a set of words they can recognise on sight. Children are unlikely to benefit from or need drilling or decontextualised activities in order to learn them.

The *Framework for Teaching* (1998) contains a list of almost 200 high-frequency words that should be known by the end of year 2 and the guidance suggests that these are best learned in the context of individual and shared reading activities. As they are words that appear in a great many books for young readers it is likely that most children will learn to recognise the majority of words on the list through normal reading and writing activities.

Children can be helped to remember words if teachers draw their attention to their distinctive features such as length, whether the word is short or long and appearance, which includes the pattern and place of ascenders and descenders. If additional practice is required in order to learn important words it can be provided through board games and writing activities. To be most effective word-level skills need to be taught at the appropriate time, when children need them, and in an appropriate way, when they are likely to be remembered. They need to be taught as part of a balanced approach which includes introducing children to grammatical and semantic strategies and which makes reading relevant and enjoyable to young children.

## *Developing word recognition*

- Play areas and activities such as construction can be resourced with words the children will read regularly.
- Draw a large road with chalks in the outdoor play area and make street and road signs for it.
- Play games such as lotto, snap and pelmanism with significant words and words that are relevant to young children's interests and

lives, such as their names, family words, TV characters, toys, food and pets.

- Use sets of words to draw attention to initial letters, rhymes and letter patterns.
- Read texts that include repeated sequences of words.
- Use shared writing to write texts with repeated sequences of words.
- Identify and discuss important and unfamiliar words in a text before asking children to read.
- Give children memorable texts to read.
- Build up a sight vocabulary of known words through reading and rereading familiar stories.
- Make books which contain words that are repeated frequently, such as 'I use my hands to help my mum', 'I use my hands to play . . .'.
- Ensure that the print-rich environment of the classroom is used as a resource for looking at words.
- Make displays of words that are topical or important.
- Teach children spelling strategies such as *look, copy, cover, write, check* which encourage the visual examination of words.
- Use guided reading sessions to discuss interesting or unknown words.
- Organise a word hunt by asking children to look for a particular word in their books and other written materials.
- Compile a list of words that have similar meanings. For example, ask the children how many words they can think of to describe *talking*.
- With the children, compile lists of words that can be used as a resource during topic work.
- Put groups of words on to a concept keyboard for children to play with and use.

## Sentence-level key skills

### *Understanding grammatical knowledge*

The way in which words are put together and ordered is governed by rules which are known as the grammar of a language. Word order in English is an important device for signalling meaning. Changes in word order usually signify a change in meaning. For example, 'The boy saw the kitten' carries a different meaning from 'the kitten saw the boy'. The number of grammatical structures is limited and repetitively used. All children develop an implicit awareness of the grammatical rules as they become speakers and listeners and are able to apply their understanding of grammar to their reading. They demonstrate this when they substitute incorrect words which are from the same word category as the unknown word when they make mistakes in their reading (Clay, 1969). When children are encouraged to apply their knowledge of how oral language works to written language they can use their sense of grammatical appropriateness to predict unknown words in text. For example in 'She . . . in the puddle', the missing word is likely to be a verb rather than an adjective or noun. When knowledge of the appropriate type of word is used in conjunction contextual understanding predictions of words are likely to be even more successful and in the example above lead to predictions such as such as *sat, jumped* or *fell*. Knowledge of grammatical appropriateness does not only apply to parts of speech but also to tense and number. This can help children to read new versions of partially recognised words easily. For example children may be familiar with *help* but not *helping* or *helped* but may be able to read these using their awareness of grammatically appropriate words.

Written language is generally more complete than oral language and often uses particular grammatical and stylistic forms for dramatic effect, such as 'said he' or 'once upon a time'. Knowing that this is a feature of print is helpful when reading, as the reader can predict groups of words that follow expected grammatical patterns. It is important to draw children's attention to these ways of using language that are particular to the written form as they often differ from children's existing experience of oral language.

## *Developing grammatical knowledge*

- Give children experiences of listening to and discussing poetry, fiction and information texts, to develop their awareness of book language and the style of written language.
- Provide opportunities for them to hear books being read aloud to give them a feel for the way words are grouped in written English.
- Invite children to join in with refrains to give them an understanding of book language.
- Suggest to children that they read on or read the sentence again from the beginning when they are reading aloud to focus their attention on what they are reading and enable them to predict unknown words.
- Work with cloze passages which contain chunks of text with whole words taken out to encourage children to use meaning to give them the information they need to find appropriate words to complete the text.

- Make books that contain repeated language structures such as 'I like my brother, said David', 'I like crisps, said Alice'.
- Ask children to check the accuracy of their reading by attending to whether it makes sense grammatically.

## Text-level key skills

### *Understanding bibliographic knowledge*

This means knowing about written texts, the way they are structured, the way language is used and the information provided by the different parts of a text. It also means becoming aware of the vocabulary that is used to talk about print and reading, such as *letter, page, title* and *author*. Use of bibliographic knowledge develops through the reader's experience of books and can be taught and demonstrated to young children by the teacher. Young children need to be aware that in English words are arranged from left to right and from top to bottom on the page. They need to be aware that it is the words that are read but that illustrations and diagrams provide valuable information for readers about the events, setting and contents of a book. Illustrations can clarify meaning and provide detail beyond that contained in the words and may also supply clues to unknown words in the text. The style of the illustrations may indicate whether stories are realistic or fantasy. Layout can indicate whether the book is concerned with fiction, fact or poetry. Knowing that the title usually suggests the content of the book helps to orientate the reader before the book is opened and helps to establish appropriate expectations which can inform predictions about vocabulary and language structures. For example, it is fairly clear from titles such as *Willy the Wizard* (Browne, 1995) or *Amazing Insects* (Mound, 1993) what each of these books might be about. The synopsis provided on the book cover provides additional clues for the reader. All this information provides a way into a book, sets up expectations in the reader's mind and allows other reading strategies to be used more efficiently.

### *Developing bibliographic knowledge*

- Story times, when children see and listen to the teacher introducing books, authors, words and letters are an important source of learning about bibliographic knowledge.
- Discuss the information provided by illustrations.
- Read the illustrations in books before beginning to read the text.
- Use wordless picture books to tell stories.

- Introduce the vocabulary needed to talk about reading when sharing books with children.
- Make sure children become familiar with the text by reading the title, author name and other bibliographic information before beginning a new book.
- Help children to understand they can make choices about books they read by using the information on the cover and the end pages and by reading the illustrations.

## *Understanding contextual understanding*

This refers to the overall meaning that is conveyed through writing. Children's previous experience as speakers and listeners and as participants in story readings lead them to expect that units of language make sense. Readers make sense of texts by using their knowledge and experience of the world, language, books and the subject-matter in conjunction with the words on the page when they are reading. Attending to the meaning of the text and drawing on prior experience to understand what is being conveyed can help the reader to make informed predictions, appropriate to the meaning of the text, about unfamiliar words that are encountered. For example, completing the sentence 'She rode her . . .' with the word *button* would show a lack of attention to meaning; however, substituting the word *bike* or *horse* would be contextually appropriate. Children's miscues often reveal that they are paying attention to context when they read and although they make might make mistakes these retain the meaning of the text. Substituting *home* for *house* in the sentence 'She went to her friend's house' would be an example of this.

Applying contextual understanding to the reading of unfamiliar words and texts is helped when used with bibliographic knowledge, grammatical knowledge, graphic knowledge and phonic knowledge. Using all five strategies can help readers to produce accurate attempts at words that are proving difficult and means that informed guesses can be made more quickly than if, for example, a word is analysed into its constituent sounds, built up and then pronounced. For example, recognising the word *castle* in the sentence 'The prince went home to the castle' could be supported by each key skill in the following ways:

- *contextual understanding* – where princes often live;
- *bibliographic knowledge* – illustrations depicting the prince entering a castle;
- *grammatical knowledge* – the word is a noun;

- *graphic knowledge* – previous experience of words beginning with *c*; and
- *phonic knowledge* – the sound produced by the letters *ca*.

The developing meaning of a text provides the reason and the reward for reading, so ensuring that children understand that texts are composed of coherent stretches of language that are meant to be understood is vital if children are to learn what reading is, what it is for and what it can do for them. If activities do not make sense they are generally rejected since they hold little interest for learners. Children who hesitate over each word, pause at unknown words, wait to be told what to say or analyse many of the words they are reading into phonemes before reading them, are unlikely to make much sense of what they are reading. Reading slowly and with too much attention to accuracy distracts the reader from the context and interferes with the ability to use sense-making strategies. In order to avoid this teachers should defer their teaching and discussion about letters and words until after the act of reading to and with children. Teaching at this stage can interfere with the flow of the text and obscure its meaning and cause children to lose the context cues that are provided when the reader focuses on understanding the meaning of the whole text.

## *Developing contextual understanding*

- Encourage children to use illustrations as a source of information.
- Make links between books and the children's own experiences.
- Provide children with lots of experience of different types of texts.
- Ask children to read the sentence from the beginning if they get stuck on a word.
- Remind children to read beyond the unknown word in order to get a sense of the whole sentence.
- Ask children to use their previous experience to guess an unknown word.
- Discuss the title, cover illustration, story or author notes before embarking on reading.
- Provide children with sequencing activities related to familiar stories.
- Produce story maps of texts used for shared reading to make the action of the story clear.
- Provide tapes to accompany popular books and information texts to support children's concentration on the meaning of what they are reading.
- Provide props that enable children to recreate stories through imaginative play.

- Create a new ending for a story making sure it takes account of the earlier parts of the plot.
- Encourage children to predict what will come next during book-sharing sessions.
- Watch story videos.
- Use resources that correspond with children's experiences and understanding.
- Use story props to recall, retell and extend familiar stories.
- Provide collections of objects for children to use to retell and revisit stories.
- Base drama sessions on known stories.
- Use the TRAY computer program which develops and requires all the key skills of reading.
- Encourage children to reread their own writing and drafts composed during shared writing sessions to consider the sense of what has been written.
- Refrain from correcting the miscues children make during reading when these do not affect meaning.
- Supply unfamiliar words during reading sessions rather than teaching word or phonic skills on the spot to ensure the sense of what is read is maintained.
- Ask the children to compile a quiz related to a known book.
- Ask the children to design a poster which conveys what the book is about.
- Establish a class book containing book reviews of some of the books children read.
- Ask the children to make resources for the imaginative play area that will enable them to re-enact stories.
- Involve children in making story props to be used alongside audiotapes and books to facilitate retellings.

## Summary

Working on the key skills of reading in ways that relate to texts and make sense to children can help young readers to understand that

- text is constant, the words on the page carry a consistent meaning;
- the text and the illustrations have different but complementary functions;
- language is composed of separate words;
- the English writing system follows a particular set of conventions;
- words are composed of separate sounds or phonemes;
- letters in words are connected to speech sounds;

- it is necessary and helpful to recognise some words on sight;
- some important and commonly occurring words do not necessarily follow phonic rules or contain features which make them easily distinguishable;
- common spelling patterns in prefixes, suffixes and roots help with decoding and establish meaning and grammatical status;
- knowledge of language helps to identify what kind of a word will fit into a particular slot;
- the language and construction of written texts share similarities with but are different from spoken language;
- knowledge of the world and the subject-matter of a book can be used to recognise words and construct meaning when reading;
- using larger text structures such as the title, headings, a table of contents and an index and knowing how texts are constructed around characters, settings, beginnings, development and endings helps support understanding of what is read; and
- using information from non-linguistic clues such as illustrations helps readers to recognise moods and consequences and understand meaning beyond the literal.

A full and varied curriculum for reading that introduces children to all the key skills shows young readers that reading need not be difficult since it involves applying existing knowledge as well as developing and using new ones. Children learn not to become overdependent on a limited number of strategies; instead they learn how to combine information from a number of sources and to understand what they read. This makes reading more accessible to children. It helps them to enjoy their early encounters with books and later to read fluently, accurately and with understanding.

## Conclusion

In order to become readers children need to develop confidence in their ability and acquire positive attitudes towards reading. They need regular, sustained and meaningful encounters with books and other forms of text. They need to become aware of and use a range of reading strategies and they need to appreciate that reading is about understanding what an author is trying to communicate. Introducing children to the key skills of reading through enjoyable and purposeful activities that are related to books will help them to learn to read and discover the pleasure that is associated with becoming literate.

# Further reading

Goswami, U. and Bryant, P. (1990) *Phonological Skills and Learning to Read*, Lawrence Erlbaum Associates, Hove.

Redfern, A. (1996) *Practical Ways to Teach Phonics*, Reading and Language Information Centre, University of Reading.

Wade, B. (1990) *Reading for Real*, Open University Press, Milton Keynes.

# 3

# Range and response

## Introduction

Range refers to the National Curriculum requirement for children to be given 'extensive experience of children's literature and reading for information using a range of sources' which 'stimulate the imagination, create enthusiasm and extend children's understanding and experience' (HMI, 1996, p. 9). Response and the use of books are learned through activities that are planned around the books and other materials children read in school and these activities will largely be determined by the resources that are available. The ways in which children are expected to respond to and use texts are explained in the programme of study for English (DfE, 1995).

As with other aspects of teaching reading, selecting resources is dependent on the teacher's knowledge. In the first place teachers need to know what is available but their choices also need to be informed by their knowledge of the uses of reading, their understanding of the key skills and their concern to motivate children so they become lifelong readers. This chapter is intended to provide readers with a rationale for selecting books for children and suggestions about activities that can be used to develop children's use and understanding of texts.

## The role of the text

One of the major tasks for teachers is to develop a class full of avid readers who use books in and out of school. Children need to acquire a love for reading that is not dependent on extrinsic rewards such as praise from adults or becoming a level-3 reader. They need to appreciate reading for its own sake by recognising its relevance to their own learning and leisure pursuits. Another of the teacher's tasks is to develop thinking readers who are able to understand, analyse and evaluate the range of written material they encounter. This enables children to use their reading ability effectively. If teachers can develop a genuine love of reading and a responsive approach to reading in the early years they will have done a great deal of what is required for children to become successful literacy users in the short and the long term. One way teachers can address both these aims is by carefully selecting the books that are to be used in school.

## Stories

Stories have always acted as a resource for introducing children to reading because all children have some understanding of oral or written stories when they begin school. Experience of stories is not only learned through listening to or reading books but it is also acquired as children hear those around them relate personal stories concerning everyday events. By the time they start school children will be familiar with using narrative to share experience. Through talking and listening to others children will have learned how to order and connect a sequence of events taken from their own experiences and to fashion them into stories. Introducing children to reading, by providing them with story books, builds on what children already know about the way narrative works and helps them to make connections between oral and written language.

Stories also have value in their own right. The popularity of fiction and the number of fiction books for all ages published each year are testimony to this. Stories offer readers opportunities to enrich their lives personally, socially and linguistically. They provide readers with a means of re-examining familiar experiences and feelings, discovering different perspectives, entering unfamiliar worlds and appreciating the power and beauty of language. The pleasure a good story can bring suggests that many children will find fiction motivating and through this develop positive attitudes towards reading. This is another reason for giving stories a central place in the reading curriculum.

Texts need to help children to learn to read and to learn about reading. Whilst all texts can help children to see the connections between oral and written language, recognise a vocabulary of words that occur regularly in print and use bibliographic conventions, some books support the children's use of the key skills of grammatical knowledge and contextual understanding more successfully than others (Meek, 1988). In the main these are drawn from the books that have been written because their authors care about what young children read and about how books are written. Such writers express their commitment to books and to children through producing 'meaningful, memorable and rewarding' texts (Ellis and Barrs, 1996) expressed in carefully considered, sensitive language.

The *Framework for Teaching* (DfEE, 1998) supports a literature-based reading curriculum which necessitates one text being reread and reused many times. To retain children's interest and support such intensive scrutiny, the books selected by teachers need to contain significant content and reveal something new at every reading. Texts that play such an important part in children's reading development need to be selected with care by knowledgeable professionals. The planned use of a range of texts as suggested in the framework presents teachers with an opportunity to appraise their existing books and select new ones using their knowledge about reading so that they can offer children a rich and stimulating reading diet.

The overall range of stories that are offered to children need to meet a number of important criteria. These include:

● being relevant to young children's lives, concerns and interests;
● containing meaningful, memorable and rewarding stories;
● supporting the application of all the key skills;
● widening horizons; and
● providing material to reflect on and discuss.

Story collections should include books that cover the range outlined in the programme of study and the *Framework for Teaching*. These include stories which

● have familiar settings
● have imaginary or fantasy settings
● are written by significant children's authors
● are retellings of traditional folk and fairy stories
● are drawn from a range of cultures
● contain patterned and predictable language
● contain challenging vocabulary
● are of different lengths.

## Traditional stories

Traditional tales are given a prominent place in the *Framework for Teaching* from reception to year 3. The books selected should include single stories and anthologies. The collection should demonstrate how stories are told within different cultures and will benefit from including classical and eastern fables, myths, legends, classic epic and comedy, animal fables, fairy tales and stories where animal characters in contemporary settings are used to explore human relationships and issues. The many traditional and contemporary tales that exist means there is the potential to compare old and new versions. The collection can be used to introduce children to cultural histories, language change and language variety. The immense number of books available in this category means that teachers can afford to select what they consider are the best ranging from traditional tales such as *The Three Bears*, to contemporary classics such as *Rosie's Walk* (Hutchins, 1968), superbly illustrated traditional stories like *Anancy and Mr Dry Bone* (French, 1991) or contemporary, humorous and more demanding texts such as *A Fairy Tale* (Ross, 1991).

## Books without words

Wordless picture books are often considered to be most appropriate for beginning readers as they can be read without having to recognise text. They can teach children about how books work, directionality, reading the contextual cues provided by the illustrations and story structure. However the quality and detail contained in the illustrations of many wordless books and the subtlety of the stories mean they can be read by experienced as well as inexperienced readers. *The Snowman* (Briggs, 1978), *Window* (Baker, 1991) and *The Tooth Fairy* (Collington, 1995) all merit reading and rereading.

## Novelty books

Young children are always attracted to novelty texts which contain pop-ups, flaps, cut-outs, split pages and hidden pictures. These can be used to motivate and interest children in reading. They can also provide young readers with valuable lessons about reading. They strongly encourage active reading strategies such as predicting what is hidden, checking guesses and reading the illustrations carefully. No early years classroom would be complete without *The Very Hungry Caterpillar* (Carle, 1969), *Where's Spot?* (Hill, 1980) or *Dear Zoo* (Campbell, 1982).

## Picture books

Books written for young children by modern authors cover a range of genres and styles. They can include realism, fantasy, adventure, school stories, animal stories, self-discovery and historical fiction. The pictures that accompany these narratives cover a huge variety of illustrative styles. Picture books introduce children to the elements of good and enduring stories including theme, issues, character and plot development. Some picture books contain sophisticated narrative techniques such as graphic, linguistic and intertextual devices. Very often the aim of these books is to entertain the reader with visual and verbal tricks and jokes. Anthony Browne and John Burningham are particularly expert at exploiting the potential of the illustrations in order to add additional meaning to the words and the Ahlbergs are justly famous for the way in which they play with the subject-matter of other texts. Not only do such books delight readers but they also encourage active reading and reveal different levels of meaning each time they are read through their use of figurative language, rhyming couplets, speech bubbles and illustrative surprises.

## Longer texts

As children gain more experience as readers they enjoy exploring stories that contain more complex plots, language and style. Many picture books can challenge readers too, for example, *Piggybook* (1986) and *Zoo* (1994) by Anthony Browne and *Enchantment in the Garden* (1996) by Shirley Hughes. However because longer books contain more text than picture books they are able to develop character and present plots which have many twists. They can provide children with a more sustained textual read than picture books. Their length, the number and type of illustrations they contain and text features such as lists of contents, chapter headings or short-story titles extend children's reading skills. Some longer reads appear in a series all written by one author or in publishers' sets of books that are similar in appearance but written by different authors. From time to time some children enjoy reading their way through a series. Just like adults, children sometimes find satisfaction in reading books by an author they can rely on or about a familiar set of characters or plot. When selecting longer books for young children it is important to consider the conceptual level of the ideas that are explored in the book and the language used. Although some books seem appropriate for more able young readers, to be understood fully they sometimes require greater experience and understanding of the world than most young children have. Whilst it is important not to take children away from the riches of picture books too soon, some longer reads are suitable for young children. These might include the 'Julian' books by Ann Cameron, the 'Happy Families' series by Allan Ahlberg and the books about 'Mouse and Mole' by Joyce Dunbar.

## Poetry

Young children are enthusiastic explorers of language and highly attentive to patterns, sounds and rhythms. A wide selection of poetry stimulates their interest and enthusiasm for language. It can also make an important contribution to their literacy learning. The relationship between oral and written language and phonological awareness can be understood as children say and read patterned language. Poets intend their writing to be heard as well as read and so rhymes and poems make excellent material for reading and saying together in shared and group reading sessions.

Poems can describe, argue, narrate, create characters, amuse and shock. They can be found in rhyming stories such as *Each Peach Pear Plum* (Ahlberg and Ahlberg, 1984), rhyming nonsense in, for example, *The Cat in the Hat* (Dr Seuss, 1961) or they may be non-narrative and non-rhyming. They may use language to create visual and verbal patterns. The poetry available for children should cover the range of poetic forms and show language being used in a variety of poetic ways. This will include finger rhymes, nursery rhymes, songs, jokes, contemporary poems, poetry from different traditions and cultures and poems by children.

Sometimes poetry can be enjoyed by readers who experience difficulties with reading or who find longer texts daunting. It can be used to tempt and give confidence to inexperienced readers since rhymes and repeated words or refrains support children's memory of texts, recognition of words and phonic strategies. In particular joke books, nursery rhymes and short poems can provide children with a way into reading. If there is a wide range of poetry available individual poems can be introduced to children regularly during story sessions where they can be linked with the themes and content explored in stories.

## Plays

Scripted plays are ideal for group reading sessions. They need to be read aloud by a number of children. Children have to follow carefully what others are reading in order to know when to read and can use intonation as they imagine their character. Some plays include parts that are deliberately unequal in reading difficulty. Play reading also gives children experience of another form of literature and introduces them to drama.

Before children are given plays to read with each other they need to be introduced to their conventions. Stage directions do not need to be read aloud but help the readers to create a picture against which the action and dialogue takes place. To help children read fluently and easily time needs to be spent on looking through the play, identifying characters and discussing the plot prior to reading aloud. The teacher can also take the plot of a play script she intends the class to read as a starting point for unscripted drama sessions to familiarise the children with the content.

## Information texts

Traditionally we have thought of children learning to read by listening to and then beginning to read stories. However it is clear that not all children have an immediate empathy with fiction. Recent research has suggested that some children, particularly boys, might find it easier to begin to read and to recognise the value of reading if they are introduced to non-fiction texts from the earliest stages (QCA, 1997). Many children will have been introduced to reading before school through factual print found in the environment such as shop and street signs, print on the TV screen and reading alphabet, number and caption books which help children to label items that are familiar to them. All children need to be able to understand and use non-fiction texts and to be able to read computer screens, teletext and information on paper that is presented in a variety of formats ranging from TV listings to advertisements. Both the programme of study and HMI (1996) recognise that it is important that young children's reading should extend beyond narrative and that they are introduced to a broad range of non-fiction texts.

Non-fiction books make use of a broad range of types of informative writing including descriptions, explanations, classifications, comparisons and contrasts, procedures, persuasive and historical accounts. Genre theory (Littlefair, 1991) has drawn educators' attention to the variety of non-fiction texts that exist and created an awareness of the range of strategies that readers need to employ to understand fully the vast array of information that is presented to them. In and out of school readers need to be able to understand and use texts that are written in the following genres:

- *Report*   a description of the way things are. Examples include reported events, observations and life-cycles.
- *Procedure*   instructions and details about how to do something. Examples include directions and recipes.
- *Explanation*   reasons for a natural phenomenon or a description of how something works.

- *Exposition*   the presentation of a point of view with evidence.
- *Argument*   the presentation of several points of view and evidence.
- *Account*   a narrative detailing past events.

Each genre has its own characteristics. This might be the use of the present or past tense, particular vocabulary items such as *first* and *next* or the structure of the text. Reading information texts also calls for the skills and experience to read diagrams and charts and understand technical vocabulary. Children need support to read and use non-fiction so that they can use their reading to learn (Mallet, 1992; Neate, 1992). With very young children it might be appropriate to use fiction as a way in. For example, *The Truth about Cats* (Snow, 1995) is a humorous book that makes deliberate and playful use of a whole range of text types, using some of the conventions of factual writing to present fictitious subject-matter. Reading and discussing this with children could lead to a great deal of learning about the style and structure of information books.

When selecting information texts teachers will want to consider whether the books contain up-to-date subject-matter, accurate facts, clear structural devices such as a table of contents, index, glossary, headings, subheadings and captions and a range of helpful illustrations including diagrams and photographs. Teachers will also want to provide alphabet books and friezes, word books, dictionaries and encyclopaedias. In addition the provision for information texts may include materials such as a local A–Z, maps, newspapers, magazines, recipe books, identification books on birds, flowers and other subjects and the children's own written instructions and accounts.

## Big books

The usefulness of enlarged texts in the early years reading curriculum was first demonstrated by Holdaway (1979). He described how reading stories using books that are big enough for the print to be 'seen, shared and discussed' with groups of children can

- display the skill of reading in use;
- encourage children to imitate and join in with literate behaviour;
- create non-threatening conditions for learning;
- promote quiet intense concentration; and
- foster non-competitive and corporate learning.

Although some publishers have been producing big books for almost 20 years, there were, until recently, only a limited number available. The support for big books given in the *Framework for Teaching* (DfEE, 1998) has led to increasing numbers of enlarged texts coming on to the market. Some big books are large versions of popular children's books such as *Not Now Bernard* by David McKee (1980) and *Where's My Teddy?* by Jez Alborough (1992). Others are produced as part of a reading scheme. Poems, songs, information texts and stories are all available in big-book format.

The criteria for selecting big books are the same as for all books, but it is perhaps even more important that they are of the highest quality. They will be used many times over with large numbers of children to teach about reading as well as to teach children to read and at each reading they will need to remain stimulating, rewarding and relevant. At a functional level they need to contain text and illustrations that are large enough to be seen by the whole class.

## Core books

Some schools choose to base their reading programme around a core of carefully selected books. Core books are drawn from the best litera-ture and information texts that are available for young children and are selected by each individual school staff. Each school's collection will be different as staff can choose the books that embody their ap-proach to reading and are relevant to their children. Each class and each year group may have access to different sets of core books to cater for different reading abilities. Multiple copies of each core book are kept in each class and used for group reading, quiet reading, reading with story tapes, retelling with story props and thematic work. The children can make models, collages, their own story props, tapes and games based around the books. They can be used as starting points for drama and promoted through posters and reviews pro-duced by the children. Enlarged texts of some of the core books may also be available or made in class by the children or the teacher. The aim of working with core books is to familiarise children with a lim-ited number of texts in order to develop their understanding of books, narrative structure, book language, the relationship between spoken and written language and a sight vocabulary. The repeated encoun-ters help children to succeed at reading, develop confidence and see reading and books as meaningful and enjoyable. Core books are not intended to be the only books read by the class, but they are often the ones that are used most frequently.

## Reading schemes

The alternative to books written only for children's enjoyment or use are those written to teach children to read and published as reading schemes. Reading schemes have attracted a great deal of negative criticism over the years. Objections to them have included their bland, limited and uninspiring content, restricted and impoverished language, dull illustrations, institutional status and uniform appearance. They can emphasise competition, make a distinction between learning to read and reading and delay or limit children's exploration of the rich treasury of books written especially for them to enjoy and in so doing constrain children's understanding of what reading can be. They may also mislead teachers and parents into thinking that it is the scheme that teaches reading. By believing that all that is important is moving through the scheme and measuring progress by the reading scheme book that the child is able to read, some adults may be deceived into thinking the scheme indicates not just how well children read but also how they will succeed at school and in life.

Of course just as not all authored books written for children are of high quality, neither are all scheme books unenjoyable. Publishers have made immense efforts in recent years to address the criticisms that have been levelled and many involve reading experts and well-known children's authors and illustrators in the production of new schemes. Particular efforts have been made to update the content of stories, provide attractive illustrations, use natural language and ad-dress equal opportunity issues by including non-stereotypical female and black characters in the books.

While some of the individual books in schemes may be enjoyable, many of the books do not compare well with books written for chil-dren to read. They tend to concentrate on telling stories about every-day events and few scheme books successfully evoke an emotional response in the reader. They continue to be constrained by using only a limited number of words in each book, particularly in those for inexperienced readers. Some schemes are also restricted by deliber-ately introducing words that can be used for phonic practice. Illustra-tions are often used to compensate for the sometimes thin content. A survey of some recently updated and new schemes (Skelton, 1997) has revealed that despite their claims publishers have a long way to go in successfully tackling equal opportunities.

One of the teacher's many roles is to widen children's reading expe-riences and give them the skills and understanding to make choices about what they read. This can be difficult if reading at school is closely linked to a scheme. However varied schemes are they cannot match the range of content and pictures available in individual books written for children since they are written by a limited number of authors. The results of a recent piece of research examining young children's ownership of books (Weinberger, 1996) revealed that the majority of children's books in the home were those bought from supermarkets. These are very often similar in appearance and structure to reading scheme books. This finding suggests that in order to widen the range of books children read, schools have to consider their provision carefully and include recently published high-quality individually authored books.

Whilst reading schemes may help teachers to create adequate readers there is no evidence to suggest that their use, either in the past or now, which has been and continues to be widespread, supports teachers' endeavours to persuade the majority of children that reading is a worthwhile and important activity. They do not guarantee success as some children have found it difficult to learn to read even when using a scheme, and they do not always broaden experiences or introduce children to the delights of reading. As HMI (1996) have suggested, children's reading should not be limited by a reading scheme. All books for reading need to be chosen thoughtfully so that children are given a positive and relevant introduction to reading through encountering texts that are involving and intrinsically satisfying.

A short description of some widely used and recently published reading schemes follows. This is intended to help readers to become familiar with schemes and consider what they offer to the reading curriculum.

## Cambridge Reading, Cambridge University Press, first published 1996

Contributing authors include Tony Bradman, John Prater and Gerald Rose. The material includes traditional stories, rhyming texts, fantasy, real life, counting books, non-fiction, cassettes, computer software, phonic games and workbooks. There are story and information big books for reception to year 2. In appearance the books are fairly uniform and feature the Cambridge logo on the front cover. The scheme is intended to teach phonics and a sight vocabulary.

## Collins Pathways, Collins Educational, first published 1994

The series editors for the scheme are Barrie Wade, Hilary Minns and Chris Lutario. The material includes big books, audiocassettes, fiction, non-fiction, poetry, plays, fantasy and real-life stories, folk tales, wordless books and a CD ROM.

### *Flying Boot, Nelson, first published 1994*

The series editor is Ted Wragg. The scheme has big books for the introductory stage, audiocassettes, CD ROMs, story and information books. The stories are about a set of children and fantasy characters. The scheme emphasises reading skills, particularly phonics and the acquisition of a sight vocabulary of 100 words. The books have a uniform appearance.

### *Literacy Links Plus, Kingscourt Publishing*

The resources include big books, posters, boxed sets of books, cassettes, phonic resources, traditional stories, real-life fiction, non-fiction, rhymes and poems. The scheme is intended to teach phonic knowledge and the acquisition of a sight vocabulary.

### *Longman Book Project, Longman, first published 1994*

The series editor is Sue Palmer with contributions from Wendy Body and Bobbie Neate. Authors of the books include Martin Waddell, Jacqueline Wilson and Adele Geras. The materials include fiction, non-fiction, big books, audiocassettes and software. The material can be used to teach all the key skills.

### *Oxford Reading Tree, Oxford University Press, first published 1985 and regularly updated*

Roderick Hunt has written much of the core material which consists of stories about a limited set of characters. The scheme also has wordless books, poetry, big books, audiocassettes, videos, software and CD ROMs. It is intended to teach key words, phonic skills and rime and analogy.

### *Reading 2000, Oliver & Boyd, first published 1994*

The scheme consists of real-life, fantasy and humorous stories and non-fiction books, some of which have been commissioned from well-known authors. It is combined with age-appropriate sets of selected Puffin books by established authors. Audiocassettes accompany some books.

### Story Chest, Kingscourt, first published 1981

Most of the books have been written by Joy Cowley and June Melser. The materials include big books, cassettes, fiction, rhymes, plays, maths and science books. This was one of the first schemes to include big books.

### Storyworlds, Heinemann Educational, first published 1996

The contributing authors include Diana Bentley and Dee Reid. The materials consist of big books, fiction and non-fiction books and cassettes. The books are colour coded and uniform in appearance. The scheme supports a key-words and phonics approach to reading.

### Sunshine, Heinemann, first published 1989

The materials consist of stories, plays, non-fiction, myths and legends, religious stories, history and geography books and big books. The books are all similar in appearance. The material emphasises a whole-word approach and the number of words on each page of the early books is limited.

## Choosing books

All classes throughout the early years will need books for beginning readers, inexperienced readers who still require support and readers who are developing independence. In order to cater for children's needs and tastes the books will be drawn from a broad range of different styles, genres and formats. Fiction and non-fiction, poetry and plays, anthologies and books by single authors and stories originating from different countries and periods can all be included.

Not every book that every child reads needs to be a classic, but as more than 7,000 books for children are published each year and there are approximately 40,000 children's books in print, teachers can be selective about the books they buy and recommend to children. Whatever sort of text, fiction, poetry, play, reading scheme or big book is being chosen teachers should evaluate each one rigorously. Teachers' will have their own particular requirements but the following list suggests some general criteria that can be used when making their selection:

- Is the external appearance of the book attractive? Will it encourage the potential reader to look beyond the cover?

- Is the book well written? Does it contain something that is worth reading?
- Is it inspiring, entertaining or thought provoking?
- Is the story coherent and convincing?
- Is the language vivid yet accessible to young readers?
- Can today's readers identify and sympathise with the characters?
- Are the moral and social assumptions in the text positive and constructive?
- Are the illustrations of good quality?
- Do the illustrations enhance and support the text?
- Is it a book that children will like?
- Do I like it?

Many of these criteria will apply to selecting non-fiction as well as fiction but there are some additional considerations about the choice of non-fiction books for young children. Information texts should

- be clearly laid out;
- contain factually reliable information about the subject;
- introduce key words and technical language in context;
- include the key features of information texts such as a list of contents, index, glossary and headings;
- have illustrations, diagrams, photographs or drawings which complement, extend and explain the written text;
- be free of bias, stereotyping and misrepresentation;
- make reference to disturbing as well as cosy aspects of subjects; and
- provide unfamiliar information to extend what is already known.

## Phonics programmes

Some schools like to use structured phonic programmes to ensure they cover this area of the programme of study thoroughly. Phonics is only one aspect of reading and is learned and reinforced during meaningful encounters with books, so phonic programmes must be supplemented by attention to the broader aspects of reading. As HMI (1996) noted phonic knowledge needs to be taught in a way that ensures transfer to the reading of unfamiliar texts. Simply using a scheme to teach phonics does not mean that teachers have a clear idea about the place of phonics in reading nor does it ensure that it is well taught (*ibid.*). The most important factor for the successful learning of phonic strategies is likely to be the quality and appropriateness of the instruction children receive.

Some published materials for phonics are described in the section that follows.

## Jolly Phonics, Jolly Learning, Tailours House, High Road, Chigwell IG7 6DL

This is written by Sue Lloyd and was first published in 1992. It introduces children to the 42 letter sounds through workbooks, videos, games and other materials.

## Letterland, Collins Educational

The author of this material is Lyn Wendon. It first appeared in 1973 when it was intended for children who were experiencing difficulty in learning to read. It has since been updated a number of times and is used in many primary schools with all younger children. It introduces children to upper and lower-case letters and their sounds through pictograms and characters such as Annie Apple. The later stages introduce letter strings. Books containing stories about the letters and videos, tapes and worksheets are also available. The programme is intended to be used alongside other reading materials.

## THRASS, HarperCollins

THRASS stands for teaching handwriting, reading and spelling skills. The material and methods were developed by educationalists with an interest in special needs and first published in 1996. It was originally intended for 7–11-year-olds finding reading and writing difficult. The authors have suggested that this structured, multisensory literacy programme for teaching letters, speech sounds and spelling could profitably be used by younger children.

## Other resources

The main resources used to foster reading development in school are books and printed material, but video and audiotapes, computer programs, games, photographs, pictures and role-play equipment can all play a part in helping children to become readers.

## Audiotapes

Story tapes enable children to become more familiar with texts and enjoy them independently. The books they accompany may have been introduced by the teacher or they may be new to the children. There are a great many commercially produced tapes available but teachers, parents and children can all make recordings of books to add to the stock. If appropriate, tapes can be made in community languages. Poetry and rhymes are intended to be heard and tape recordings can bring them to life for children. Tapes can help children to develop a sight vocabulary of known words as children see and hear words when they read and listen to the text. They also foster phonological awareness.

## *ICT*

There is a growing stock of computer software available to support reading, including alphabet software, software for special needs, talking books, concept keyboard overlays and stories and information texts on CD ROM. Careful thought needs to be given to the software that is selected and how it is used.

HMI (1996) were critical of the use of some software they saw in use in schools and considered it to be of limited use. They wrote (*ibid.*, p. 15):

> Where information technology was used in the teaching of reading it was most frequently used to help children to match sounds to letters . . . The pupils generally did not go on to apply what they learned in wider reading. They did not, that is, easily transfer the skills and knowledge they had acquired to the reading of new text.

Some teachers question the value of stories on CD ROM. Whilst they may be motivating for some children they tie up the computer for long periods of time. The practice they provide can, for the most part, be gained through reading a book.

Software that is flexible and that can will remain useful over a long time is likely to be most valuable. Programs such as TRAY which can be used with any age to develop all the key skills of reading and concept keyboards that can be programmed to suit the needs of individuals and the class are good examples of helpful material. Information texts on CD ROM are also likely to be of lasting use and can support children's reading of non-fiction and the development of research skills.

## *Videos*

Videos of children's books can be used to provide additional opportunities for children to listen to and discuss stories. They can also be used for specific purposes. Before watching a video the children can be asked to look and listen for specific information about a character, the setting or the plot. After the video they can be given follow-up work such as drawing the sequence of events or drawing a character and creating speech bubbles for him or her.

TV programmes such as *Words and Pictures* and *Storyworld* which introduce stories and activities related to books and words can be used to widen children's experiences of stories and provide them with reading practice in different ways.

## Story props

Story props provide children with hooks they can use when retelling the story independently or to others. They usually consist of reproductions of some of the illustrations, characters and important objects in the text. They may also be collections of real objects such as plastic animals and a boat for *Mr Gumpy's Outing* (Burningham, 1978) or a collection of clothes and a bear for *How Do I Put It On?* (Wantanabe, 1977). These collections can be kept in the listening area, used for the children's table-top play activities or placed in the role-play area.

Some schools build up resource packs of materials to accompany popular books. These can contain story props, collections of objects, games, audiotapes and examples of successful activities.

## Special events

Books on their own do not teach children how to read. They have to be actively promoted and used. Regularly planned events can help to stimulate children's interest in books. Schools can plan a book week when there is a week of special events associated with books and authors. They can celebrate National Poetry Day, organise a read-athon or plan a school-sponsored read. Teachers and parents can share their favourite books and poems with children. There can be book displays in individual classes and throughout the school related to individual authors or illustrators, particular genres such as school stories or humorous books, and to themes such as books about friendship or toys. Activities such as these convince children of the importance of reading and do much to keep them interested in books as well as helping them to see all the different books that are available for them to read.

Information about putting on special book events in school can be obtained from School Publications, The Poetry Society, 22 Betterton St, London WC2H 9BU or Young Book Trust, Book House, 45 East Hill, London SW18 2QZ.

## *Keeping up to date*

Since one of the most important resources for reading is the teacher's own knowledge it is important to keep up to date with what is available. There are a number of helpful sources of information. Some of these are described in the section which follows.

### Books for Keeps
A journal that provides up-to-date information about children's books, authors, audiotapes and awards.

### Literacy and Learning
A journal that contains articles on practical issues related to teaching English in primary schools.

### Language Matters
A journal about English published by the Centre for Language in Primary Education.

### Letterbox Library
A book distributor providing selections of non-racist and non-sexist material, reviews and newsletters.

### National Association for the Teaching of English
Distributes two journals about reading, *The Primary English Magazine*, which concentrates on practical issues, and *English in Education*, which contains accounts of research into English. NATE also publishes and distributes books and pamphlets.

### Reading and Language Information Centre
Based at the University of Reading, the centre produces a range of practical publications for teachers.

### Signal
A specialist journal devoted to children's books and authors. *Signal* also publish their own booklists and books about reading.

### The Primary English Magazine
Distributed free to NATE members but also available by separate subscription. This is a practical journal for primary schools.

### United Kingdom Reading Association
An association that promotes and disseminates research into reading. It also publishes a journal, *Reading*.

## Developing response

Reading is an active, purposeful meaning-making activity. Planned opportunities for discussions about texts help children to realise that understanding, evaluating and using what is read are as important as recognising the words. They can encourage children to reflect on what they read, discover interests and enthusiasms, learn from their reading and learn from the interpretations of others. They will also help them to discover that reading strategies can vary according to the type of text that is being read and the reader's purpose. During response activities teachers are able to assess children's understanding, attitudes and interests.

Benton and Fox (1985) have suggested that responding to what is read involves four elements:

- *Picturing and imaging*   building up a mental picture of the character and scenes in the book.
- *Anticipating and retrospecting*   predicting events or reflecting on what has been read.
- *Engagement and construction*   becoming involved in the text emotionally or through identification with characters or situations.
- *Valuing and evaluating*   making judgements about the worth of the text or about the content.

Thinking about these can help teachers devise activities which encourage children to respond to what they read. Picturing could take place through art activities or play with story props. Anticipating and retrospection could be encouraged by making a large scene-by-scene frieze of a story. Engagement and construction can take place during drama and role play. Discussion and written activities such as keeping a personal reading diary, book reviews, debating and voting for favourite books, making posters to advertise books and writing to authors all involve children in making judgements about what they read.

Children benefit from teachers who share their own thoughts about books and their own reading with them. When teachers share ideas and impressions openly and at times other than in reading sessions they act as models and encourage children to reflect on their reading. Sometimes teachers may provide a focus for a class or group discussion. They can ask children to name a favourite book and think of two good things about it or identify a book they did not enjoy and give two reasons for this. The children might be able to work in pairs to do this activity. They need to be given time to think about likes and dislikes and will benefit from having seen the teacher model choices and reasons. The class could be invited to comment on the books nominated by their peers and to give their own reasons for agreeing or disagreeing with their choices. Class or group discussions concerned with evaluating books can be given a focus if a display of books is used as a starting point or if children are asked to read collections of book reviews and then write one themselves.

During discussions teachers will want children to talk about their reading, exchange opinions and analyse the content and issues contained in the books. To do this they will elicit initial responses to the subject-matter, the characters, the setting and the plot. They may ask children whether what they have read reminds them of anything within their own experience or other books they have read. To explore the book further teachers may ask the children to examine the author's use of language, the choice of words and images. They may ask the children whether any words or phrases caught their attention and to explain why. The next stage may be to look at the structure of the book. To help children to think about how books are organised teachers can ask them to identify the parts they found most important and what they were thinking about as they were reading. Then the group can look at the way the plot develops and identify significant events. Issues and ideas can also be explored.

Children also need to be shown how to read, use and evaluate non-fiction texts. Teachers can begin to do this during shared and group reading sessions using information texts. Shared writing can also be used to draw attention to the features and structure of different text types. Investigating written material such as maps, packaging and environmental print draws attention to how words are arranged in different ways to suit particular purposes.

The following section provides some suggestions for activities that encourage exploration and response. They may be used with the whole class, groups, pairs and individual children. Some may be undertaken in shared writing sessions or during teacher-led group work. Others may be suitable for children to undertake independently.

## *Responding to fiction*

### *Activities to explore characterisation*

- Write a list of likes and a list of dislikes about the main character;
- design a birthday card for the main character;
- discuss how the characters are made to seem frightening or familiar;
- the teacher can take the hot seat in role as the central character and answer the children's questions about his or her motives and behaviour;

- retell the story with some children reading the words spoken by the characters; and
- make a collection of similar characters from other books.

### Activities to explore setting

- Make story props to retell the story;
- read the opening again and discuss where and when the story is taking place, who has been introduced, what sort of atmosphere is being established and how we know;
- demonstrate making a chart to record information using the headings *where, when, who* and *atmosphere*; and
- complete a similar chart using a different but similar story.

### Activities to explore plot

- In pairs play a game of consequences using the headings *one day, then, in the end*;
- draw a sequence of pictures to retell the story;
- act out the story;
- reread the book together asking individual children to tell a section of the story at a time;
- represent the plot in a sequence of pictures or story map; and
- ask the children to think about when the action gets complicated and identify the problem and the solution.

### Activities to explore text type

- Discuss, with reasons, whether the story is fantastic or real; and
- make a collection of books containing similar characters or events and classify them according to text type.

### Activities to relate books to children's own experiences

- Discuss personal experiences that are mirrored in the book; and
- draw or write about personal experiences that are similar to those in the text.

### Activities to encourage children to establish preferences

- Carry out a survey of favourite books about similar subject-matter;
- read and discuss other books by the same author; and
- introduce a termly top-ten chart of books.

## Using and evaluating non-fiction

### Activities to help pupils to access information

- Build up sets of information texts and other resources that can be used to support children's investigations of a topic;
- discuss what they already know about the subject-matter;
- discuss conflicting information or inconsistencies;
- consider whether what is known is fact or fiction; and
- examine the cover and consider what the book might be about.

### Activities to help pupils to read information texts

- Set a purpose for reading;
- read the book together;
- list the information it contains;
- identify unknown words, discuss meanings, consult dictionaries;
- begin to build up a class glossary;
- in pairs children use reference books to begin to compile a chart about one aspect of the topic; and
- during plenary sessions the children can report on the contents of the books they have used.

### Activities to help pupils to reorganise and record information

- Ask the children to suggest headings for a chart to record what they know about their area of investigation;
- identify what the children would like to know more about; and
- draw and label pictures.

### Activities to help pupils to share information

- Children can display their material using captions to organise it;
- children can talk to the class about their findings;
- children can produce a series of pictures, diagrams or time line to show to the class;
- the information can be entered on to a database; and
- the children can make a book.

## Conclusion

Texts are important in the reading process. The careful selection of books is crucially important to the development of reading skills and attitudes. They need to be books of quality, which introduce children to the work of skilful authors and illustrators, ideas and facts. When teachers have selected the books for their children with care they can expect children to become involved in reading and as a result to want to learn to read for their own immediate and long-term gratification.

# Further reading

Bennett, J. (1991) *Learning to Read with Picture Books* (4th edn), Thimble Press, Stroud.

Ellis, S. and Barrs, M. (1996) *The Core Book*, CLPE, London.

Lazim, A. and Moss, E. (1997) *The Core Booklist*, CLPE, London.

Mallet, M. (1992) *Making Facts Matter: Reading Non-Fiction 5–11*, Paul Chapman Publishing, London.

Meek, M. (1988) *How Texts Teach What Readers Learn*, Thimble Press, Stroud.

Sylvester, R. (1991) *Start with a Story*, Development Education Centre, Birmingham.

# 4

# Organising for reading

---

## Introduction

Organising for reading development draws on the teacher's general management skills and her awareness of the possibilities and constraints on teaching and learning that exist in early years settings. Effective organisation is also informed by the teacher's knowledge of reading. Together, knowledge of organisational strategies and subject knowledge enable decisions to be made about how best to present children with opportunities to learn.

A number of recent HMI surveys into reading and classroom practices have found that the way in which the teaching and learning of reading is organised is the main determinant of the difference between high and low achievement and that high-quality opportunities for learning which involve using a variety of carefully selected and well managed methods of teaching generally result in high standards (Alexander *et al.*, 1995; HMI, 1995; 1996). HMI John Stannard, the director of the National Literacy Project, has identified classroom management as 'one of the biggest problems in literacy teaching' (1995, p. 10). And it is clear that this concern has significantly influenced the design of the literacy hour.

A number of factors contribute to effective organisation for reading (HMI, 1996). These include:

- the length of time spent on reading;
- the way in which the time is used;
- effective classroom management;
- matching provision to children's abilities and needs;
- the way in which high-quality resources are used;
- challenging children with interesting and appropriate texts; and
- creating rich, well used literacy environments.

These considerations have to be set alongside the teacher's knowledge about reading. As HMI (ibid., p. 8) wrote, 'Changing the organisational pattern . . . will not in itself solve the problems. Teachers themselves have to be more knowledgeable and skilled about reading in order to teach it successfully'. The combination of subject and pedagogical knowledge enables teachers to make decisions about what children need to know next, find the best way of achieving teaching intentions, design teaching episodes, select and use resources and justify their choice of a particular learning route. It is what is done with knowledge, time and resources that can make a difference to how easily and how well children learn to read.

This chapter will explore some of the management issues that affect the teaching and learning of reading. These are the interpretation of subject knowledge, the organisation of activities and children, the use of time and resources and creating a stimulating and supportive learning environment.

## Subject and pedagogical knowledge

Teachers need to understand what reading is for, why it is important, the skills that are needed to read and how these develop. It is important to have a clear picture of what has to be taught before thinking about how to teach it. Teachers who have limited knowledge of a subject will find it difficult to plan and teach effectively. Previous chapters in this book have introduced readers to some of the main elements of the subject knowledge that are needed in order to teach reading.

Earlier in this book I suggested that the three models that have been used to describe reading each lead to different teaching approaches. It is also true that teachers who in the main subscribe to one model of reading often interpret their preferred model in a particular way. They may prioritise different aspects of the model because of their own experience as readers, their understanding of the role of reading in children's lives and their own confidence in teaching some or all of the key skills. Alternative and individual interpretations of knowledge about reading affect what is taught and how teaching is arranged.

How reading is taught is then influenced by how teachers choose to work with children. During their career teachers find a preferred teaching style. They may work in ways that demand

- high adult involvement and low pupil initiative;
- low adult involvement and low pupil initiative;
- low adult involvement and high pupil initiative; and
- high adult involvement and high pupil initiative.

In a longditudinal study of the literacy curriculum, Webster *et al.* (1996) related teaching style to how children are taught about reading.

**Table 4.1** Approaches to teaching phonic skills

| Teaching style | Phonic teaching |
| --- | --- |
| High adult involvement and low pupil initiative; teaching is teacher driven | Alphabet learned by rote; basic phonic rules established first; letter combinations practised in isolation |
| Low adult involvement and low pupil initiative, teaching is resource driven | No direct teaching of the alphabet; phonics-based reading schemes used to introduce phonic rules; structured reading materials used to introduce blends |
| Low adult involvement and high pupil initiative; teaching is pupil driven | Children given experience of books before the alphabet is introduced; phonic rules understood through reading; phonic blends not taught while children are reading |
| High adult involvement and high pupil initiative; teaching is learning driven | Alphabet discussed in relation to names, signs, labels and children's questions; phonic rules taught as children read; phonic blends discussed alongside picture clues, word shapes and reading on |

They found that the choice of teaching style and classroom practices leads to differences in the way in which reading is taught and organised in the classroom. Table 4.1 summarises some of the variations that emerged when teachers with different styles of teaching were asked about their approach to teaching phonic skills.

This research suggests that, on its own, subject knowledge does not determine the quality or appropriateness of the teaching children receive. It illustrates how decisions about the quantity and type of learning opportunities children are given are affected not just by teachers' knowledge about reading but by their choice of teaching style. All the teachers in each of the four categories recognised that phonics was an important aspect of learning to read but provided for it in different ways.

There are some important and timely lessons to be learned from this piece of research. The *Framework for Teaching* (DfEE, 1998) advocates a teaching style that demands a high level of teacher involvement. Using the models identified by Webster *et al.* (1996), adopting this style could lead to either a teacher-driven or a learning-driven approach. The former results in a curriculum where skills are emphasised, the latter in developing the key skills in the context of meaningful reading experiences. Teachers who are implementing the requirements of the framework have to make choices about how they will teach the key skills. Ideally the choice of approach should coincide with what is known about reading and learning. The role ascribed to children will also influence the decision. In the teacher-driven model pupils are largely passive receptors of information. Where the emphasis is on learning the pupils are far more active. The teachers in this category encouraged pupils to take risks, to view mistakes as normal and to collaborate with others as they learned.

Although the *Framework for Teaching* (DfEE, 1998) offers very detailed guidance on the content and structure of the curriculum there is sufficient flexibility for teachers to decide how they will teach the key skills. They still have the freedom to consider how they will organise the classroom to support learning, to design activities that give children opportunities to learn as well as to be taught and to decide on the type of support they give to children. They can also select the resources to be used and decide how these will be presented to children. Reflecting on teaching style and thinking about the process of reading present teachers with the opportunity to make choices about the exact way they teach and develop reading, to create congenial contexts for learning and do far more than deliver a curriculum.

## Managing teaching and learning

Teaching and learning in the early years take place during whole-class times, teacher-directed group sessions, independent group work and individual pupil activities. One of the aspects of the teacher's role is to use the teaching arrangements that are available to ensure children learn. This means that the selection of teaching strategies needs to be combined with knowledge of what has to be learned so that children are presented with appropriate learning experiences. Teachers need to create opportunities for extending pupils' achievements through direct intervention and organise productive activities that involve and interest children in their own learning.

The *Framework for Teaching* (DfEE, 1998) places a great deal of emphasis on the teacher working with the whole class and groups of children. Both can be efficient ways of organising children and ensuring all the children in a class receive direct teaching. However the use of a particular method does not automatically guarantee that children are taught well or that they learn. It is the match between what has to be learned and what takes place within the particular arrangement that can make a difference to learning.

Teaching can include any of the following:

- instruction
- demonstration

- explanation
- questioning
- giving feedback
- discussion
- participation.

All of which can take place with the whole class, groups and individuals. Different teaching strategies are appropriate for different aspects of learning and for different pupils at particular times.

Learning does not just happen when children are receiving direct teaching; it can also occur through

- exploration
- rehearsal
- observation
- practice
- consolidation
- extension
- revision.

The teacher's knowledge of the children's present level of experience will inform her choice of the learning opportunity needed and will shape the activities and the teaching provided.

The decisions made about teaching arrangements, techniques and activities should ensure that suitable conditions and situations for learning are created in the class, since how something is taught can significantly influence what is learned. Arranging teaching and learning episodes involves the teacher in applying a range of professional skills. Organisation is not merely a question of managing pupil numbers but of catering for a range of individual and important learning needs.

## *Whole-class work*

Whole-class teaching makes it possible for teachers to instruct, model and explain clearly to large numbers of children. This is an efficient way of working when introducing new learning all the children require and when the learners are motivated and interested in what is being taught. During whole-class sessions teachers often ask challenging questions, ensure children attend to what needs to be learned and give feedback about the quality of work (Galton, 1995). At its best teaching is clearly focused and well paced. When children are stimulated and challenged through high-level exchanges whole-class work is effective. However there are limitations to whole-class teaching.

During class sessions it is not possible to establish exactly what each individual child is learning – for example, some children, although appearing to listen, may not be fully attending or understanding. There is also a tendency for whole-class teaching to be pitched at the middle of the ability range in the class and so it does not always cater for the needs of the more or less able children (Alexander *et al.*, 1992). While whole-class sessions are a useful way of introducing and demonstrating new learning they need to be followed by teaching that meets the specific needs of the children in the class.

## *Group work*

Effective teaching can take place with the whole class, a group or individual children if the characteristics of good teaching, which include maintaining pace, asking challenging questions, providing clear explanations and giving feedback related to the task and the learner, are employed. However, Galton (1995) noted that these techniques are less commonly employed when the teacher is working with small numbers of children because her involvement with them is often interrupted by other members of the class. The children who are working without direct adult supervision, on group or individual tasks, often seek support from the teacher and prevent her from teaching effectively. These demands for information, many of which are trivial, can result in children spending less time on their work as they wait for the teacher's attention and the teacher using valuable time to manage rather than teach pupils. In this situation it is not possible for teachers to extend learning through sustained, high-quality discussions either with the children she has planned to teach or those seeking help.

What is required are classroom procedures and routines that foster children's independence and minimise the managerial demands on the teacher's time. This is important because teachers do need to spend time with groups and individuals in order to provide responsive teaching that meets children's learning needs. While whole-class instructions and explanations are appropriate for teaching children general routines, skills and facts, other forms of teaching, such as helping children to apply new learning, to solve problems and engage in discussion, are more suited to teacher-directed groups. When working with groups the teacher is able to match her teaching to the needs of individuals. She can support children at different stages of development by tailoring her explanations and the difficulty of the activities. Through questioning and discussion she can discover exactly what the children know and can do, clarify individual misunderstandings, reinforce learning and extend present abilities: 'the difference between good and bad reading teachers is . . . to do with their sensitivity in matching what they do to each individual child's learning needs' (DES, 1975, para. 7.20, p. 106).

Productive group work can pose problems and, for those not used to this form of organisation, it can seem quite daunting. This is because whilst the teacher is working with one group the remainder of the class are working without direct adult supervision. The problem is how to make sure the children who are working independently remain on task and do not interrupt the teacher. The solution is to establish routines for the children to follow and to plan the activities children undertake without adult attention with care.

Routines that support children's autonomous work arise from the teacher's expectations about how she wants the class to work and the procedures she explains and reinforces with the children. Young children can and do concentrate for extended periods on activities which they find satisfying and when they have access to the materials they need to sustain their involvement. Children can be engrossed in the imaginative play area, with construction materials, in the writing area and when using the computer. These activities are generally resourced appropriately, the children are clear about what they are doing, there are explicit rules for the use of the areas and equipment and teachers expect that children will enjoy and remain with these activities for long periods. If these conditions are reproduced for other activities most children will work seriously and carefully at completing their tasks.

Fostering autonomy begins with expecting that this is possible and then explaining the rules and procedures that support independence to the class. Children need to know that they do not interrupt the teacher when she is working with a group unless their query is important. This needs to be reinforced by the teacher's behaviour. If children do look for adult attention unnecessarily they should be reminded of the rules. The resources children need to consult and use should be accessible to them. They should know where they are and how to use them. Many materials such as books and pens can be placed on tables; others, such as tapes, story props and books in the listening area, can also be prepared before the children begin their work. This helps children to settle quickly and pre-empts requests for help in finding equipment. Before beginning their work the children should be clear about what they have to do, how they will set about it and why they are doing it. It is likely that the teacher will have explained this during whole-class times and will reinforce it at the end of sessions when children from each group share their work with the class.

The teacher can also encourage the children to see their peers as a resource for learning and for solving problems. Again this can be explained but, more importantly, it can be reinforced by designing activities that foster co-operation. Children do not have to undertake individual activities when sitting in groups. They can work in pairs to complete a sequencing activity, sort words or identify and make a collection of spelling patterns. When they are familiar with group reading and have some fluency with reading they can read as a group or use the guidelines for group reading to read with a partner. Working co-operatively helps classroom organisation since the children can consult one another if they have problems but more importantly it can benefit children's learning. When working with others children have to articulate what they know and ask questions to clarify uncertainties. The answers they are given by peers are likely to be phrased in a way that makes sense and the dialogue that ensues can help both children to reflect on the activity and their understanding.

Effective group work, like all successful teaching, depends on thorough planning that takes account of the abilities of the children and the nature of the task as well as rules, routines and resources. Work that is too difficult will result in interruptions for the teacher as the children will need to seek help. Work that is too easy will also lead to disruptions because the children may become bored or finish quickly and they will then find other, possibly noisy, ways of occupying their time.

When planning for groups the teacher can consider the ways children learn. She can decide whether children need to be given exploratory, practice, consolidation, extension or revision activities. This will depend on what they already know, and what they have done previously. Children who have successfully used a set of sequencing cards to retell a story may be ready to make their own set of pictures showing the main events in the book. Other children may be able to write the text to accompany their set of illustrations. It may seem easier to give children who are working without an adult practice or revision activities as they will have used the knowledge required to complete these before. But giving children too many activities that are familiar and lack challenge wastes opportunities for extending learning and may lead to bored and disruptive learners.

Finally the teacher will consider how many self-directed groups will be at work at any one time, how many children will be in these groups and how children will be allocated to groups. Teaching groups may best be arranged by comparable ability so that similar learning needs can be addressed together. Other groups can be arranged according to friendship, gender, deliberate mixed ability or randomly. The composition of the groups can be changed according to the task. The number of groups at work on different activities should be manageable, four or five are the ideal but when self-directed activities such as the use of role play or story props are used it possible to have more. Group activities can include work in the listening area, with language games, on the computer and in the imaginative play areas. These need less supervision than even well devised pencil-and-paper activities and by planning for their productive use the teacher will be reducing the number of potential demands that may be made on her time.

Quality teaching and learning depend on the careful application of pedagogical expertise. The selection of a particular teaching strategy and the choice of techniques that are employed in whole-class or group work need to be matched with knowledge about the development of reading. Careful planning and preparation are then needed to ensure the teacher's skills at developing children's learning are used to best effect.

## Time

The majority of teachers, whatever their experience, often feel there is too little time in the school day to teach every child everything they need to know in the best possible way. This is particularly true when teachers are discussing reading. In a survey which asked 100 teachers about their use of time in school Campbell and Neill (1994) found that many teachers expressed serious concern about the time they could give to reading. The number of hours children spend at school is limited; this is unalterable, so teachers have to think of ways in which they can use the time available to maximum effect. A number of research studies have been undertaken into how time is used in classrooms during sessions concerned with developing literacy. The findings from these studies offer some suggestions about how teachers can organise their classes and themselves to create more time for teaching and more opportunities for learning.

The ORACLE (Observational Research and Classroom Learning Evaluation) studies (Galton *et al.*, 1980) were undertaken in 60 primary and middle schools and offer some interesting insights about the way in which teachers use their time in the classroom. They found that

- a great deal of time that could be used for teaching is spent on managerial tasks;
- many of the teacher's interactions with children were unrelated to work; and
- on average teachers spent less than 10% of their time on reading.

It is surprising that so little time was spent on reading. However this finding is partly explained by the other points extracted from Galton *et al.*'s findings. Time that could have been given to reading was spent on managing children, answering questions and explaining the requirements of tasks rather than on teaching children how to read more effectively. Teachers may have intended to spend more time on reading but were distracted by managerial problems and so lost teaching time.

However as the authors of the report on the National Curriculum at Key Stages 1 and 2 (NCC, 1993, p. 17) wrote, 'what is important is not ultimately the quantity of time: it is, rather, the quality of teaching and learning'. They then refer to the Leeds study (Alexander, 1991) which found that language work was sometimes of poor quality because too much time was spent on it. Other studies have also examined how the time spent on learning is used. Bennett *et al.* (1984), when considering the nature of the tasks teachers provided for children, found that

- the majority of tasks involved children in rehearsing familiar routines and known concepts. They were given little new knowledge and large amounts of practice; and
- only approximately 40% of the allocated tasks matched children's abilities.

More recent research (Webster *et al.*, 1996) has revealed that it is the frequency, depth, quality and purpose of children's encounters with literacy that make a difference to what is learned. They have suggested that it is when teachers sustain high-quality learning opportunities using well chosen and carefully managed teaching methods that pupils achieve well in reading. Focused teaching that addresses pupil needs and tasks that challenge pupils not only to apply their skills but also to extend them are needed to ensure learning and progress.

The literacy hour may ensure that teachers spend more time on teaching children how to read. However there are two other significant considerations. First, as the research studies show, it is the quality of the teaching that is important; and, secondly, by thinking that learning about reading only occurs in the dedicated hour, teachers may neglect to plan for reading in other areas of early years provision.

Quality of teaching depends on giving children the information they need to improve. This varies between children, so the teacher has to be alert to individual needs. Catering for these depends on the teacher's knowledge of the children in the class, her understanding of the way they learn and their exact requirements. It also depends on her understanding of all the strategies that enable children to read, how these can be made clear to children and her understanding of progression in reading. A reading programme that includes the frequent use of activities that keep children busy may not be well matched to individual need, may not extend children's repertoire of reading strategies and may not stretch their present understanding. It may keep children occupied and may appear to be concerned with the teaching of reading but it is not necessarily the best way to ensure learning. Worksheets are an example of this type of activity. They give children something to do but rarely teach them something new. HMI (1996) were critical of the widespread use of worksheets as a means of teaching reading. They commented that they require undemanding responses, are time consuming and present children with a series of low-level tasks and, through their use, 'Much potential teaching time was simply wasted' (*ibid.*, p. 16).

Early years practitioners know that children can learn in a variety of situations. Learning about reading does not only take place when teachers are directly working with pupils. Story times, play activities, writing and other curriculum areas can all make valuable contributions to learning to read. Literacy experiences outside school also support learning. These may include children reading books that are borrowed from school with adults but might also be times when they are reading from computers, reading teletext from a TV screen, reading library books and engaging in informal real-life reading and writing episodes with carers. All this means that teachers need to plan for reading in crosscurricular and extracurricular activities. They need to see the possibilities for reading in all activities and provide appropriate teaching and resources. They should also find out what children are learning outside school and provide information and resources to support these experiences. This extends provision for reading, time spent reading and will help to develop and consolidate children's reading.

What can be done to use time effectively?:

- Establish calm, orderly pupil behaviour to keep managerial interactions to a minimum.
- Have clear teaching intentions which focus interactions and children's learning.
- Establish routines that enable children to work independently.
- Match activities to pupils' learning needs.
- Use teaching procedures that are most appropriate to what is to be taught.
- Use whole-class and group teaching for some aspects of teaching.
- Have a manageable number of activities some of which require minimal supervision.

- Carefully plan how teaching time is to be used.
- Give children realistic deadlines for the completion of work.
- Consider the balance of exploration, practice and extension work children are given.
- Exploit all learning opportunities by planning for reading across all curriculum areas.

## The physical environment

A carefully prepared and well maintained physical environment can make a significant contribution to the literacy curriculum. It can

- support and reinforce children's literacy learning;
- act as a resource for children's independent work;
- be a source of productive literacy activities; and
- signal the contribution reading can make to our lives.

Displays, reading and writing centres and play areas are common-place in early years classrooms and because they are regarded as such their role as real and important resources for learning can be over-looked. They can make a significant contribution to children's learning. The way classrooms are arranged, what is displayed and the resources available to the children can reinforce the skills the teacher wants the children to learn, encourage independence, provide oppor-tunities for children to explore and consolidate reading and demon-strate how reading is used in the world outside school.

One of the most frequently used spaces in the classroom is the carpet area where the children and the teacher gather three or four times a day to talk, read, share books and write together. Because this space is used so often it is important to make sure it is arranged to suit the teacher's and the children's needs. There should be sufficient room for all the children to sit comfortably and to see the teacher easily. A bookstand for displaying enlarged texts and a flip chart should be available and visible to the class. Many important literacy lessons are learned when children are seated on the carpet and it is worth spend-ing time thinking about how it can best be organised and what items of equipment it needs to contain.

All classrooms should have a book area or library and, as this sig-nals the status the teacher gives to reading, it should be arranged and maintained carefully. It should contain a wide variety of books that are attractively displayed. It is better to have fewer books that are displayed well and changed regularly than too many books that are untidily arranged, uncared for or too tightly packed into the shelves to be easily accessible. The condition of the books needs to be monitored regularly and books may need to be repaired, thrown away or re-placed at intervals. The books can be organised into fiction and non-fiction. The non-fiction can be categorised further if teachers wish to include reference material such as dictionaries and thesauri. The books that have been made by the present members of the class should also be stored in the book area and displayed in the same way as commercially published texts. Enlarged texts and books used for group reading can also be placed in the book area so that children can return to known texts at quiet moments on their own. Teachers may wish to separate group readers from the main body of the books in the area by placing them in storage boxes as the whole set may need to be accessed quickly. Having extra copies of books used for group reading can be helpful. They can be placed on the library bookshelves so that the children can read or borrow them and the group reading sets can be kept together. The book area can also house comics, magazines, local newspapers, telephone directories, an A–Z of the area and a book in which children can write comments about the books they read.

The children will use the book area to browse through books, refer to information texts, read alone, share books with a partner, borrow books to read at home and hear stories read aloud. The way the books are arranged and involving children in its organisation will support their independent use of the area and help them to become familiar with the books that are available. It will also contribute to their ability to make choices about the books they want to read. Teachers might want to devise rules for the use and maintenance of the area with the class and display these on posters. A well organised book area will support the children's efforts to keep the area tidy. The children should know the system for taking books home. They may be able to record their choices and take responsibility for changing books them-selves. Good organisation should mean that children use the area regularly and it should save the teacher time.

In many classes the listening area is adjacent to the book area. As both are quiet spaces and as tapes and books can be stored together in the reading area this often makes good use of space. The listening area may also contain a magnet board on which the children can arrange story props as they listen to the story. Puppets and collections of other items that support the children's retellings of stories they hear and read can also be stored nearby. The children can use the tape recorder to record their own stories and commercially produced texts which then become additional resources for the class to use.

Every classroom should contain a writing area that is well supplied with paper, envelopes, card, Sellotape, scissors and other resources that encourage children to write. Blank books in different sizes, book-making equipment, notepads, diaries, a visitors' book and calendars invite children to experiment with writing in different ways. Writing reinforces learning to read by giving children practice with letters, words, expressing meaning through print and exploring written formats. The area can also contain reference materials such as displays of letters, writing styles and scripts in many languages, alphabet books, simple dictionaries, word lists, a noticeboard and suggestions about what to write.

This should be an area children can use independently and purposefully. They can write for their own purposes, at their own pace and without needing adult attention. They will be helped to do this if they are shown how to use the resources and are involved in organising the area. Working with the teacher, in shared writing sessions, they can compose notices and labels for the equipment. Some of the writing produced in the writing area can be shared with the class, responded to or displayed.

Imaginative play areas are an important resource for all of sorts of learning in the early years classroom and need to be organised as carefully as any other planned learning activity. Adding literacy materials which encourage children to read and write provides opportunities for them to explore print in many forms. Books, magazines, brochures, telephone directories, calendars, diaries, maps, notices, forms, notepads, paper, envelopes and a range of writing implements all have a place in the play area when it is used as a home, café, shop, garage, office or library. These scenarios help children to understand the uses of literacy in the world outside school, to see literacy as a normal part of existence and to apply their developing reading skills in realistic ways. The area can be given a more imaginative focus by transforming it into a scene from a familiar book. If it is resourced with a few well chosen props it can be used by children to re-enact familiar stories and explore plot and characterisation. For example, a crown and a few cloaks could be used by the children to take on the roles of Princess Smartypants and her unfortunate suitors (Cole, 1986). The children's use of resources is helped when adults spend time modelling literate behaviour in the play area. The children will imitate adult writing and reading behaviours and incorporate these into their play. To remain effective the focus of the role-play area and the resources that are used should be changed regularly. Involving the children in making changes and preparing props to be used in the imaginative play area encourages them to use the resources effectively and prompts discussion and reflection on reading and books.

The ICT area can also be resourced to support reading. Simulation games, text disclosure programs, databases and CD ROM format books all encourage reading and exploration of text. New software can be introduced to small groups of pupils who can then be given responsibility for showing other children how it works. When children work together in this way the teacher can save time and the computer becomes a resource for independent work. Concept keyboards familiarise children with words, help them to remember a set of key words and are a useful spelling resource.

Art and creative activities can provide children with opportunities to explore books further. Children can respond to books through drawing, painting, making models, producing maps and collage. Publishers' posters of books and authors can be displayed in the art area and can be used to discuss different illustrative styles.

The remainder of the classroom, tables, chairs and equipment need to be arranged in ways that facilitate the children's easy access to resources. The children need to be familiar with what is available and where things are kept. Tables and chairs should be arranged to facilitate collaborative group work. The fact that children do sit in groups should be capitalised upon and the phenomenon of children always working alone even when grouped around a table avoided. Displays of work, artifacts and books all support reading. They contain print that can be read and used by the children when they write. The children can make some of the labels and captions for displays or write explanations to accompany their own work. This provides them with extra experience with print and provides reading material for others. In early years classrooms collections of environmental print and the children's names are particularly valuable when displayed and used as they can provide a meaningful way into print for all children.

## Children

Classrooms where reading is good are orderly places where children are engaged in appropriate and involving tasks (HMI, 1991). When children are clear about the teacher's expectations and her routines they are more likely to settle quickly and contribute to the calm, purposeful atmosphere of the classroom. Children enjoy being busy rather than having nothing to do and appreciate interesting activities when these are arranged for them. Purposeful activities rather than those designed merely to occupy will sustain children's concentration for longer and make a greater contribution to their learning. If the classroom ethos encourages independence and collaboration the children are likely to initiate and extend their own learning through using the reading, writing or imaginative play areas. If all the opportunities for literacy development are to be used by the children, it is vital that the children are confident and feel happy to have a go at reading and writing without waiting for the teacher to instigate this or give her permission. All the children in the class have a right to the teacher's support but, when the class is noisy or unsettled, the teacher's attention is usually given to a few children and rarely contributes to their learning. For this reason teachers have to attend to issues of management and control if they are to teach reading successfully.

## The contribution of additional adults

Careful thought should be given to the way in which assistants are deployed in school. They can make a valuable contribution to children's learning and to the smooth running of the class. In order for their work to be effective teachers should give them clear guidance about the nature and purpose of the activity, the expected outcome and their role. In the weekly planning for the class teachers need to consider which activities should be allocated to the classroom assistant and indicate this. There should be a system in place for classroom assistants to share their observations about children's development with the teacher. Volunteers can also be an important resource in the class. The time they spend in school and the effective use of this time should be considered when teachers are planning.

It is essential that the teacher makes sure all the adults she works with are aware of their role and respond to children in a way that corresponds to the ethos of the class. Untrained but willing helpers may think they are being of most help if they give children the answers to questions that are set or supply unknown words quickly when children hesitate as they are reading. They may believe that telling rather than allowing children to think and attempt to discover answers for themselves is the most effective way to teach and ensure children learn. The teacher may need to explain that controlling children's thinking can reduce the possibilities for learning since it does not allow children to consider possibilities, explore alternatives or draw on previous learning. People who work in schools are united by their wish to develop children's learning and are grateful for advice on how to this. If explanations about routines and expectations are given when they first begin to work with the children, adults are unlikely to be offended and more likely to pleased at being given clear guidelines about their work.

Although the prime focus of this book is on organising for reading in school teachers may want to take account of the work parents and carers do with children at home. If the school has a well established home reading programme many children will receive practice in reading outside school. In her planning the teacher may want to take account of children who have less support at home so that additional opportunities are provided for them in school. She may also consider the sorts of activities children do at home and suggest that these are varied from time to time to support children's particular learning requirements.

## Conclusion

Effective organisation that supports high-quality teaching and effective learning in reading is likely to occur when

- the classroom atmosphere is calm, orderly and quiet;
- teaching is focused on learning;
- teaching is informed by an understanding of reading;
- routines and structures contribute to children's learning;
- time is given to whole-class, group and individual teaching;
- whole-class, group and individual teaching are matched to what is to be learned;
- space inside and outside the classroom is used well; and
- all who work with the class understand the teacher's aims and approach.

When thought has been given to the organisation and management of teaching, learning, children, time, the environment and additional adults the specific teaching of reading is more likely to be successful and effective.

## Further reading

Alexander, R., Rose, J. and Woodhead, C. (1992) *Curriculum Organisation and Classroom Practice in Primary Schools*, Department of Education and Science, Stanmore.

Galton, M. (1995) Do you really want to cope with thirty lively children and become an effective primary teacher? In J. Moyles (ed) *Beginning Teaching: Beginning Learning*, Open University Press, Buckingham.

HMI (1990) *The Teaching and Learning of Language and Literacy*, HMSO, London.

# 5

# Routines and activities for developing reading

## Introduction

This chapter offers readers a description and a rationale for some practices which can be used for the teaching and learning of reading in all classrooms. There are many ways to offer children opportunities to learn how to become readers. For many years reading was mainly taught through individual reading sessions where children were heard to read by the teacher. In recent years however, this practice has been questioned and criticised. Sessions are often too short to identify reading needs or provide children with the help they require and, because they are often interrupted, do not demonstrate the enjoyment that should be associated with reading. HMI (1993) commented that the value of reading to the teacher lies in the quality of preparation and follow-up work in which the individual reading session is embedded and that frequent, brief individual reading sessions make this difficult. More recently HMI John Stannard (1995, p. 10) has said: 'Of course one-on-one teaching is a very good way to teach, but it is totally impractical in a class of 30.'

Worthwhile teaching does not only take place when individual children read aloud to an adult. There are other ways of organising which enable teachers to spend longer periods of time with children and provide them with quality teaching and learning opportunities. The routines described in this chapter provide a context within which specific aspects of reading can be taught and learned. The key skills of reading need to be taught within a planned programme that brings literacy alive for children and provides them with opportunities to extend their existing knowledge about oral and written language. This is necessary if children are to be stimulated by reading and read now and in the future with enthusiasm and enjoyment (DfE, 1995).

The way in which the routines in this chapter are used each day and across a whole week will differ in different classes. The age of the children and the teacher's preferred style of organisation will affect which activities are used and when. All the activities described can be incorporated into the literacy hour. They can also be used outside this time and in classes that arrange their literacy teaching in other ways. Many of the suggestions can be used in early years classrooms, where teachers organise a number of activities that are available for children throughout the school day. The descriptions that follow are intended to help teachers select those which are most appropriate to their situation.

## Modelling literate behaviour

### *When and with whom*

This should take place as frequently as possible with all children.

### *Why*

Children learn from listening to and watching skilled adults read. Demonstrations of reading are a way of explaining and demystifying the activity of reading. They show what reading can do for readers and how readers read. Teachers who value and enjoy literacy for its own sake can show children the purposes and pleasure to be gained from reading. They can convince children that reading is worth while. Teachers who

- talk about their own reading;
- openly and informally ask children about their reading;
- discuss books with children;
- listen and respond seriously to children's opinions and questions;
- participate fully and collaboratively in class, group and individual reading sessions; and
- provide children with meaningful encounters with print

contribute a great deal to children's reading development. Teachers provide a role model that has a powerful influence on what children learn about reading. All the routines outlined in this chapter depend for their success on teachers' commitment to reading and to helping children to learn to read in the most productive way.

## Shared reading using big books

### *When and with whom*

With the whole class and with groups, once a day. This is suitable for all ages of children from the nursery onwards. Groups of children benefit from shared reading.

## *Why*

When using an enlarged text with groups or the whole class all the children can see the print whilst the teacher reads. As the adult reads the book she is modelling the skills and strategies used by readers and introducing children to the conventions of written language in narrative and non-narrative texts. Children can see how books work and how the different parts of a book contribute to the reading experience. The text and illustrations can be discussed and the children respond to what they have seen and heard. Later the children are invited to join in the shared reading. When they join in, their collaborative reading allows them to learn from each other.

The support provided by the teacher reading aloud enables all the class to gain experience of reading the whole text even those who are only able to recognise a few words. This provides children with a coherent, substantial and non-threatening introduction to reading. In this way the children become familiar with the text and develop confidence in their ability to read. Repeated readings extend confidence and enable the children to read the large book or smaller versions alone or with a friend, initially using their memory of the text and the illustrations and later by combining their knowledge of the content with their increasing sight vocabulary.

Although enlarged texts and shared reading times can be used to teach children about books and reading skills it is important not to let the teaching of reading take priority over the enjoyment of books. Stories, in particular, need to be read and savoured for their own sake not reduced to the level of instruments for didactic teaching. Shared reading should reinforce children's understanding of the delights and satisfactions of reading. During shared reading sessions the teacher is modelling reading behaviour to the children. Normally readers read a complete or a sustained piece of text without interruption. Sometimes teachers interrupt their reading to the class with inappropriate questions and comments about the text. Gregory (1995) has shown how confusing this can be for inexperienced readers who can be misled about the purposes and procedures involved in reading by this behaviour. Discussions about the way the book has been written, its language, organisation and structure and examining words and conventions of print should take place after or before the book is read.

## *How*

- Introduce the book, discuss the cover and the title and invite the children to make predictions about the story;

- read the story;
- reread the story and invite the children to join in;
- make the book available for independent reading; and
- use the book as a starting point for follow-up activities which explore the text further.

## Guided group reading

### *When and with whom*

One or two groups every day. Inexperienced and more experienced readers can benefit from this activity as the examples that follow illustrate.

### *Why*

Guided group reading enables a teacher and a group of children to read, talk and think their way through a text. It helps children to learn reading strategies and to respond to what they read with and, later, without, the teacher's support. Reading aloud with others and sharing knowledge, strategies and ideas help children to read with expression and intonation, to support and listen to each other and to express their own opinions about what they read.

### *How*

The groups need to be small, about four to six children, and contain children at roughly the same level of development. If the group is too big or some of the children experience too many difficulties the group may become bored or impatient. The most suitable books for group reading are fairly short stories or plays matched to the children's abilities. It is also a useful way of introducing children to reading information texts as time can be spent discussing the arrangement of the book and individual children can be asked to search for particular items in the text. Ideally each child should have a book but one between two can work. Teachers can introduce group reading by being part of the group, joining in and taking their turn. They can encourage children to help each other and read with expression. In this way the teacher acts as a model that the children will eventually be able to imitate without always needing the presence of an adult. The following list contains suggestions about what might take place during a guided group reading session:

- introduce the book;
- discuss the cover and title and make predictions about content;

- with beginning readers the teacher reads and the children follow the text;
- with experienced readers each child and the adult read one page at a time aloud;
- with more experienced readers the children can read silently before moving to the next stage;
- discuss the story, evaluating it, reflecting on it and making comparisons with other books;
- draw attention to words and letters; and
- extend the story through follow-up activities and links with other books.

What follows is an example of a guided reading session using *My Book* (Maris, 1985), with beginning readers. Throughout the episode the teacher is teaching the children a great many things but she does not interrupt the meaningful enjoyment of the story. Overt teaching is saved until after the reading has been completed:

| *Teacher strategies* | *Teaching points* |
|---|---|
| Look at the cover. What can we see? | Familiarises children with the content |
| Look at the words. Put your finger on the first word. It says . . . and the next word says . . . So the title is . . . | Bibliographic information; meta-language – title, author; word recognition of key vocabulary; directionality |
| Open the book. Look at the words inside the cover. Teacher reads these. | Meta-language – cover, words; connecting written and oral language |
| Look at the next page. The words say. | Repetition of key vocabulary |
| Turn over. What can we see? | Familiarity with the book which will help with understanding and predictions |
| Reads the dedication. | Connecting oral and written language |
| Turn over. What can we see? The words say . . . Makes links between picture and words. Turn the flap. What can we see? | Developing sight vocabulary; the helpful role of illustrations |

| | |
|---|---|
| Turn over. Where are we now? And the words say . . . | Sight vocabulary |
| We have followed the cat from the garden to the gate, to the door. Where do you think we'll go next? Turn the flap. | The unfolding of the story; prediction; bibliographic knowledge |
| Turn over. Where are we? What do you think will be through the door? So what do the words say? | Prediction, contextual understanding; encourage children to read |
| Turn over. Where might we be now? Why do you think that? | Read the illustrations; prediction |
| Turn the flap. Which room are we going into? Were we right? Whose bedroom might it be? How do we know? What do you think the words say? | Reading the illustrations; prediction; preparation for reading; encouraging children to read and identify words |

The book is then read to the end using similar teaching strategies. The following example shows the teaching that can take place during a discussion after the reading:

| *Teaching strategies* | *Teaching points* |
|---|---|
| So whom does this book belong to? How do we know? | Inference using the pictures |
| What was the cat doing? | Inference using pictures; exploring the way the book works |
| Have you got any special books? What are they? | Relating the story to the children's experiences |
| Did you like the book? Why? | Encouraging children to express and justify opinions |

After the discussion the teacher could read the book again and invite the children to join in when they can or this second reading could take place the following day. This reinforces the story and the sight vocabulary. After the second reading the teacher might use the following strategies:

| *Teaching strategies* | *Teaching points* |
|---|---|
| Let's look at the cover. Can anyone point to the word that says *Book*? | Reinforcing sight vocabulary |

| Can anyone find another page where we can see that word? | Reinforcing sight vocabulary; encouraging children to attend to details and the shape of whole words; graphic knowledge |
| --- | --- |
| Does anyone know the sound of the letter at the beginning of *book*? | Phoneme–grapheme correspondence |
| Can we find any other words that begin with *b*? | Reinforcing phonic awareness |

Follow-up work could involve the children in drawing all the items in the book that begin with *b* and labelling these using the book as a spelling aid. The writing and drawing could be incorporated into a 'B' book to which further *b* words could be added. The book could also be used as a starting point for making a collection of words that sound like book or bed to extend phonological awareness. It could also be used as a stimulus for children to write a 'My Book' of their own. The children might be encouraged to find other books by Ron Maris or the teacher could read a book written by him at story time.

With more experienced readers the teaching strategies and teaching points will be different as the following example using *Dave and the Tooth Fairy* (Williams, 1993) shows:

| *Teaching strategies* | *Teaching points* |
| --- | --- |
| What is this book called? Who wrote it? What does the illustration on the cover tell us about the book? | Familiarisation with content; use of bibliographic cues; prediction, contextual information; introducing main characters |
| Teacher reads the back cover. | Prepares the children for the contents and some key vocabulary |
| Open the book. Who can read the words? Teacher reads some of the words. What does the picture tell us? | Reinforcing vocabulary; making connections between oral and written language; reading illustrations and using them to predict |
| Gives children time to look through the book to find Dave and the Tooth Fairy. | Familiarisation and preparation |

| | |
|---|---|
| We are going to read this book together. Each of us will read a page in turn. If anyone finds this hard I'll join in and help. I'll start. | Explaining the procedure; promising a sustained and satisfying read for all children, even those who might not be able to read such a long text alone at one sitting |
| Teacher reads. | Orientation, preparation |
| Children reading. | Practice; word recognition |
| Teacher and child reading together or teacher supplying unfamiliar words. | Retaining the meaning of the text; supporting children |
| Teacher asks children to guess an unknown word using the context. | Using contextual cues |
| Teacher asks children to use initial letters to help them guess. | Applying phonic knowledge and context together |
| Teacher notes words the children found difficult. | These will be reinforced after the reading |

After the reading the teacher and the children discuss the story. The teacher might ask why the Tooth Fairy had to return to Tooth Fairy-land or how Dave got enough money to buy a kite, in order to explore their understanding. She could ask what sort of a boy Dave is, in order to explore characterisation. To explore plot she could ask what would have happened if Grandad had not found the tooth.

At this point the teacher can ask the children to find and focus on specific words that had been difficult to read. These could be reinforced by identifying individual letters and letter strings, spelling them out and using word-building strategies. Words that contain similar elements could be found in the text or the children might think of examples. The teacher explains what we can do if we cannot read a word, including using illustrations, phonic clues or considering what words are appropriate to what the story is about. She makes reading strategies explicit to the children.

Follow-up work could include producing a sequel about Dave and his kite or what happened next to the Tooth Fairy in her new job. The children could decide on their sequel in pairs and record this in pictures or words. They could write a character study of Dave by drawing a picture of him and listing all the words that describe him.

# Reading conferences

## *When and with whom*

All the children in the class at least once a week. More frequently with beginning readers and children making slow progress.

## *Why*

Reading conferences are carefully planned opportunities which enable teachers to spend extended periods of time teaching, discussing and evaluating individual children's reading. They give the teacher the opportunity to observe children's reading behaviour and use of strategies, teach the use of the key skills of reading, discuss children's response to the book, their general reading interests and their difficulties, develop positive attitudes to reading, discover children's reading preferences, monitor progress and identify what each child needs to learn next.

Reading conferences can take different forms according to the experience of the reader and the teachers' intentions. They may include:

- reading the book to the child;
- reading some of the book and encouraging the child to join in;
- offering the child the opportunity to read aloud to an adult; and
- discussing the child's book and reading after listening to the child read a short extract.

The first two activities enable children to read by following the text and listening to the words in a non-threatening way. The third and fourth allow children to share their reading with an interested participant. Teachers who read with and to individuals and talk about books are demonstrating that reading to an adult is not merely a time when reading is assessed or taught but a time for enjoying and understanding books.

## *How*

Beginning readers benefit from listening to the text being read a number of times before joining in with the adult. Unfamiliar texts can transform a fluent reader into a stumbling reader. Inexperienced readers and children who have just selected a new book to read need to become accustomed to the text in order to become attuned to the language, style and content before they begin to read. This helps them to understand what they are reading and to read with greater confidence and independence.

When teachers read to a child they can

- read the text straight through;
- follow the reading with a discussion about what has been read; and
- use the book to foster awareness of words, letters and reading strategies.

With slightly more experienced readers they can

- talk about the title, content, setting, characters;
- read the first few pages of the book with the child; and
- suggest the child joins in or reads alone.

With more fluent readers the teacher may expect children to read some of the book independently but offer to share the reading if the child encounters difficulties. By sharing the reading the teacher is providing support and encouragement. Supporting readers in this way can be helpful when a child

- is approaching an important part of the book;
- is losing interest;
- experiences difficulties; and
- is reading a text written in an unfamiliar or complex way.

With independent readers the teacher can ask the child

- to discuss what he or she has read so far;
- select an extract to read aloud;
- identify any difficulties; and
- talk about his or her response to the book.

Reading aloud to an adult is the time when teachers can offer specific help and extend children's skills and strategies. During the reading the teacher responds to any difficulties the child demonstrates in a way that causes least disruption to the reading and limits her interventions to those miscues which detract from the child's understanding of the text. However by employing strategies and questions similar to those that follow she is still providing valuable lessons about reading:

- Leave time for and remind children about self-correction:

  –does that make sense?
  –do you think that is right?
  –read the sentence from the beginning and invite the child to suggest the unknown word;
  –provide the unknown word.

- Suggest strategies:

  –have another go at reading that sentence;
  –read on a little further and then see if you can work the word out.

- Look at specific words:

  –what sort of a word would fit there?
  –have a guess at the word;
  –look at the first few letters and think of an appropriate word that
    might begin with those letters.

The teacher's interventions signal and teach children about the sort of
cues that can be used when reading. She will want to indicate that
using syntactic and semantic cues through rereading and reading on
is helpful and provides the context for the use of grapho-phonic cues.

After the reading teachers can develop children's understanding of
what they read and continue to extend their reading strategies and
knowledge about language by:

- Discussing the book and fostering response:

  –what did you like about this book?
  –did it remind you of something that has happened to you?
  –do you know anyone like Grace?
  –do you know any other stories about Spot?
  –which is your favourite and why?
  –was this as good?

- Drawing the child's attention to some of the following:

  –unknown words
  –unusual words
  –particular letters
  –spelling patterns
  –the structure of the book
  –the style
  –other similar books.

During a reading conference the teacher attends to the child's confidence, independence and interests as a reader. She notes the range of
strategies the child employs and the child's knowledge and understanding of print and books, as well as encouraging the child to reflect
on and enjoy reading. She will record and use what has taken place to
inform her teaching and the substance of future conferences.

Reading conferences should be long enough for the child to read a
whole story or episode and discuss this with the teacher. Allocating
time for them depends on good classroom organisation and normal

classroom routines which support pupil autonomy and independence (Campbell, 1990). The class needs to be engaged on activities which match their capabilities, be clear about what to do when they finish an activity and know that they do not interrupt the teacher when she is working with individuals. They will occur frequently with beginning readers and with more experienced readers who are attempting to read books that are demanding or written in unfamiliar genres. They can be less frequent with more confident readers. Sometimes conferences are timetabled to take place during lunch or break times. The problem with this arrangement is that reading becomes something that takes children away from other enjoyable activities and may be seen as an extracurricular activity that does not have its own place on the timetable. This may affect the children's view of the status of reading and their attitude towards it.

# Reading partners

## *When and with whom*

Each group or the whole class to read in this way once a week. This is most suited to children in Key Stage 1 and older but can be helpful for younger children if they are paired with more experienced readers.

## *Why*

Reading partnerships provide opportunities for children to gain practice at reading extended pieces of text and receive help from others. They can be particularly valuable for less confident readers who sometimes find it easier to read to and receive help from another child rather than the teacher.

## *How*

Children choose or are allocated a regular reading partner. It can be helpful to pair children with different reading abilities and originally more and less experienced readers were paired (Topping and Lindsay, 1992). Some schools pair children from different classes. The two children in the partnership take turns in reading aloud to each other from a book of their choice. During the reading the partner can give the reader help by supplying words or the two children may try to work out unfamiliar words together. If children have not yet reached the stage of reading alone they can 'tell' the story to their partner by reading the illustrations in the text. Paired reading can take place regularly as a whole-class activity or as an activity for a group during the literacy hour.

## Sustained silent reading

### *When and with whom*

The whole class every day for increasingly longer periods as the children get older.

### *Why*

Periods of silent reading in class give children the opportunity for a sustained read from a book of their choice, enable them to see adults enjoying reading and enhance the status of reading for its own sake. In these sessions children are able to develop their experience and enjoyment of books.

### *How*

The guidelines for organising silent reading were first described by McCracken (1971). He suggested that

- a regular time should be allocated for silent reading each day;
- each child should have a personally selected book ready before the start of the session;
- the teacher should also read a book during this time;
- there should be no talking or movement around the class during the session; and
- this is a time to enjoy reading and not a preparation for future work although, after the session, some children might recommend a book which they have particularly enjoyed reading to the class.

Many teachers have found that periods of silent reading work best if they occur after a natural break in the school day such as playtime or lunchtime. Before the break the children select their book so that they are ready for the session when they return to class. Although ideally this should be a silent time, with very young children, who often read aloud to themselves, the time may be quiet rather than silent. As long as the rules of silent reading are explained to the children and it becomes a regular feature of the school day, children as young as 4 will happily read or look at a book for five minutes or more. By the time children are 7 the silent reading period may be as long as 20 minutes. Normally the whole range of books in class will be available for children to choose from but, every so often, the pattern of silent reading sessions may be varied by having a theme for the session such as information books, magazines or books by named authors.

## Story times

### *When and with whom*

With the whole class and with groups at least once and up to four times a day at every age and stage.

### *Why*

The learning that can take place during story times is enormous. They can promote children's interest in and familiarity with books and encourage children to want to read as well as providing suggestions about the books they can select to read. They can introduce children to authors and genres they have not yet explored. It is at story time that the teacher's enthusiasm for books can be transmitted authentically and regularly to the class.

During story times teachers model the strategies readers use to make sense of writing. They help children to learn early and important concepts about print such as directionality, the connection between speech and text and the meta-language needed to talk about reading. Children are introduced to expression and intonation, new words and their meanings and learn about language patterns that are more complex than those they use when speaking or encounter in their own reading. The discussions that follow story times encourage children to respond to and reflect on books and recognise that books can contribute to our understanding of the world.

### *How*

Traditionally story time occurs at the end of the day or at the end of each session in the nursery, but there are sound reasons for introducing story times at other times. When a story is introduced at the beginning of a session children can explore it further through related activities. Alternatively a story read in its entirety the previous afternoon can be discussed at the beginning of the next day and used as the starting point for a series of story-based activities. In the course of a week a teacher will probably select a range of stories that offer children opportunities for personal, social, intellectual and language development. These will be varied in content, style and length and selected for their appeal to the children in the class. The choice of books and the way in which they are read or told will do much to affect children's attitudes to books, authors and reading.

Telling and reading stories to children is a real art. One only has to listen to and watch professional story tellers to realise how inadequate one's own performance sometimes is and what a spellbinding experience it can be. Listening to and watching actors telling or reading stories on TV, radio and story tapes can provide teachers with ideas about how to share stories well. This depends not only on the use of the voice, including clarity, projection, level, varieties, intonation, pace and the use of pauses, but also on the use of a whole range of facial expressions and gesture. The range of strategies that a teacher employs to transmit the meaning of a story means that story times can be particularly valuable for children with special needs and those whose home language is not English. Incorporating some of the suggestions given in the guidelines which follow may help teachers to convince children that stories are extraordinary and make story time a truly magical time for them.

### Selecting the book

- Choose a story you like or enjoy;
- make sure you are familiar with the story;
- make sure it is appropriate for the audience;
- consider where you will be able to use sound effects, emphasis and repetition; and
- prepare and use props such as puppets or examples of items mentioned in the text.

### Before the reading

- Ask the children to look at the cover, title and author of the book;
- ask for the children's ideas about the content and the characters;
- make links with stories they have previously encountered;
- explain any words that may not be understood; and
- ensure you have the children's full attention before beginning.

### During the reading

- Do not be afraid to take a risk – children enjoy something different;
- allow the children time to respond and absorb what they hear and see;
- encourage the children to examine the illustrations to enrich their understanding of the story;
- do not rush to finish the story – pauses and silences can be very effective for creating tension and drama;

- involve the children by encouraging them to help with props and sound effects;
- if you are sharing a story in episodes, summarise what has happened so far before beginning;
- enjoy yourself and so will the children.

### After the story has been shared

- Give the children the opportunity to express their opinions and reactions;
- take the children through the illustrations again;
- provide opportunities for the children to recreate or retell the story orally;
- place the book in a prominent place in the classroom so that the children can read or browse through it at their leisure;
- if a tape of the story is available place this and the book in the listening area; and
- ask a group of children to create story visuals for the book so the story can be retold and enjoyed in a different way.

## Sequencing

### When and with whom

This is a collaborative activity that can be undertaken without adult help once children are familiar with it. Nursery and reception pupils may need more support. It can be planned as a once a week activity for groups of children.

### Why

Sequencing activities help children to become familiar with story structure and narrative language as well as offering children an opportunity to revisit books that have been introduced to them during shared reading sessions. When sentences are sequenced children will be using grammatical knowledge and contextual understanding to decide on an appropriate order as well as referring to the other key skills of reading. Sequencing also encourages rereading and prediction.

### How

Pictures and words taken from a book or photographs and sentences recounting an activity in which the children have participated, such as an experiment, a school event, an outing or a cooking session, are mounted on separate cards. These are then used by pairs of children, who work together, to arrange them in order. After the children have sequenced the cards they can use them as the framework for narrating a story or event to other children or to an adult. The children can also make their own cards for this activity based on their own favourite books or class events.

Children who are ready to explore narrative structure in a more sophisticated way can be given a set of sentences copied from a book they know and asked to arrange these in a logical sequence. To do this they will have to read and reread the sentences carefully and use clues such as the words *then* and *at last* to complete the activity. They will be drawing on and extending their grammatical knowledge and con-textual understanding.

Variations on sequencing include creating story maps and time lines related to a book and asking children to draw a favourite part of a story and then to draw what came before and after their first picture.

## Story props

### *When and with whom*

With the class or a group when used by the teacher or as a daily independent activity for pairs of children and individuals, throughout the early years.

### *Why*

Sets of props or puppets that can be used to retell a known story can give children valuable practice at rehearsing plots, sequences of events and exploring character. They can also lead children back to the text to check the details of their retelling.

### *How*

Teachers can make story props by copying or cutting out pictures of characters and significant items in stories that are shared with the children. These can be mounted on card, covered with a plastic film and a magnet or piece of Blu-tack can be attached to the back. This enables them to be displayed on a magnet board or white board as the story is being told. Initially the teacher might model how they can be used as she tells or reads a story to the class. They can then be placed in the listening area with the book and an accompanying tape for the children to use independently. When children are doing some extended work on a book they can make their own sets of story props.

## Language games

### *When and with whom*

As an independent paired or group activity that all the children can undertake at least once a week. Very young children benefit from adult guidance.

### *Why*

Making a collection of games associated with popular books can provide additional practice for children who are becoming familiar with the structure and language of stories as well as helping them to recognise words and letters.

### *How*

Snap cards can be made easily by children or adults. Two sets of identical playing cards with illustrations relating to the book on one side and the matching word on the other are needed. The first set of cards can be photocopied before being coloured in to ensure an exact match. Lotto pieces can be made in a similar way. A piece of A4 card can be divided into four. In each section the children draw a character or item relating to the book, underneath the adult writes the word. The A4 cards are photocopied before the base board and the photocopies are coloured in using identical colours. The photocopies are cut into four pieces and used to cover the lotto board when the game is played.

More adventurous track or matching games can also be produced. For example the journey described in *On the Way Home* (Murphy, 1982) could be represented as a track on which the different friends or creatures Claire encounters could be drawn. Using a die the children move along the track picking up illustrated cards that match the squares on which they land. At the end of the game each player can use his or her set of cards to retell part of the story. Words can be included on the cards that are collected to help the children become familiar with them. *Bet You Can't!* (Dale, 1987) could be the basis for a game for two players. The aim might be to see how many objects each player can put in the toy basket. The children would need a large illustration of or a real basket. All the toys illustrated in the book could be copied on to cards and given a number from 1 to 6. Using a die the children could collect the item that matches their number and place this in their basket. For very young children it might be more appropriate to use a die with colours and to colour-coordinate the cards.

Other word games such as set of snap cards with the children's names written on them and their own illustration or photograph of their face could help children to recognise important words and provide opportunities for looking carefully at initial letters and letter patterns and similarities and differences in words. Using the cards to make sets based on initial letters, final letters and word length would develop these skills further.

## Collections

### *When and with whom*

With the class or a group when used by the teacher or as an independent activity for individuals or pairs of children, throughout the early years.

### *Why*

A collection of items that are used to illustrate a text can bring story times to life. Collections are particularly useful if a book contains unfamiliar vocabulary or experiences as the objects, related to items mentioned in the text, support understanding and may extend vocabulary. They may be especially helpful when sharing an information book. After its initial use the collection can be displayed and each object labelled, to reinforce the children's developing sight vocabulary. Collections can also be used by the children to retell or re-enact the story alone.

### *How*

A teddy bear and a collection of doll's clothes could be used to accompany *How Do I Put It On?* (Watanabe, 1977). Seven teddies and a doll could support the telling of *When the Teddy Bears Came* (Waddell, 1994). A collection of decorations, crockery, food and games would illustrate *Dat's New Year* (Smith, 1995).

## Role-play activities

### *When and with whom*

Daily for groups of children of all ages, working independently.

### *Why*

The imaginative play area can be resourced with props that enable children to recreate stories they have heard, using dialogue and action to reconstruct the text. This helps children to become familiar with book language, plot and characterisation.

A set of masks which represent the different characters in a book can be used as resources in the imaginative play area and during story sessions. These could be made by adults but could also be made by the children. They could then be used in subsequent tellings. Stories in which masks can be easily and beneficially used include those where characters accumulate and participate in the action such as *Patrick* (Blake, 1968) or books which contain a limited number of characters all of whom make a significant contribution to the story such as *The Three Bears*. A basket and items of food mentioned in *The Shopping Basket* (Burningham, 1980) might lead children to imitate the story. More elaborate dressing-up resources including a red cape and a wolf mask could lead to the re-enactment of *Little Red Riding Hood*. Outside role play might be encouraged by placing masks, a teddy and a large box outdoors after a reading of *It's the Bear!* (Alborough, 1994). Children who choose to spend their time using the wheeled equipment outside could be offered chances to access literacy by setting up a garage and equipping it with car magazines and manuals, signs, receipt books and diaries.

## Prediction

### *When and with whom*

A once-a-week group activity that can be undertaken independently when children are familiar with it. With very young children it will need adult guidance and the activity will take place less frequently.

### *Why*

Prediction can encourage children to explore context and reflect on the meaning of words and the clues about reading that are contained in illustrations.

## *How*

The children are given a photocopy of the cover or first page of an unknown book. Using the information contained in the words and pictures they can be asked to draw or list who will be in the book, where it is set and what might happen. They can then check their predictions to see how accurate they were. The aim is not necessarily to get the predictions right but to see how much can be inferred from limited information if it is given thought. This activity can be worked on individually, in pairs or with the teacher in a large group.

## Cloze procedure

### *When and with whom*

A group activity that can be undertaken independently once children are familiar with it. Suitable for children who have some familiarity with reading, can recognise some words and can draw on many reading strategies. It can be used once a week for each group.

## *Why*

Using cloze procedure encourages children to read for meaning and to reflect on text. It can develop children's use of grammatical knowledge and contextual understanding.

## *How*

Individually or in pairs the children are given a meaningful extract from a book or a complete text prepared by the teacher from which a number of words have been deleted. The children's reading ability should be considered when making deletions and the number of deletions should not prevent children from making sense of what they read. The children read the passage and decide what the missing words might be. These can be inserted in the text. Sometimes the children's own writing can be used if it is word processed. The intention of the activity is to find the most appropriate words rather than just to get right answers. The emphasis is on reconstructing the text so that it makes sense.

This activity can be used to teach children about parts of speech if, for example, adjectives or verbs are deleted. It can also help children to think about individual letters, blends or digraphs if the beginning of the word is left in the text but the remainder of the word is deleted. The advantage of working on phonics in this way is that the children can use the meaning of the text to refine their phonic guesses. Phonic knowledge is being taught in a way that encourages its transfer to the reading of unfamiliar texts (HMI, 1996).

## Shared writing

### *When and with whom*

With the whole class once a week, with groups once a week. It can be used with all ages of children although sensitive awareness of children's ability to concentrate and benefit is necessary. It is important to match the type and relevance of the writing to the understanding of the children.

### *Why*

In general, learning to write supports learning to read and so all the experiences children have with writing can have a beneficial effect on their reading. Shared writing refers to the times when a group of children compose a text collaboratively, with the teacher acting as the scribe for the group. It is a way for teachers to 'help pupils to compose at greater length by writing for them, demonstrating the ways that ideas may be recorded in print' (DfE, 1995, p. 9). When children are familiar with the format they may take over some of the scribing but initially it is more helpful if an adult does this. This is an excellent way of teaching children about reading and writing in the nursery and reception classes. It can help children to make connections between spoken and written language. It can teach children about words, spelling patterns, print conventions, text structure and authorship. As the skills and practices that are demonstrated during shared writing sessions provide a model for children to use when they write, it can be used to reinforce their learning about reading by offering opportunities to think about words and letters and to reread what has been written. It teaches children about the permanence of text and about how writing helps people to remember ideas and how reading can recover these thoughts. Less confident readers will see others making mistakes with words and benefit from seeing that their peers and the teacher do not always have a perfect grasp of literacy at the first attempt. Shared writing can also be used with older children as more sophisticated genres can be introduced, demonstrated by the teacher and practised by pupils.

## *How*

Shared writing sessions are generally best organised by having the children sitting on the carpet and the teacher writing on large sheets of paper on a flip chart or an easel. It can be undertaken with the whole class for writing that is of interest to all the children such as a letter to be sent home or the final results of an experiment. With a new class it is best to begin with a simple piece of writing. Alternatively it can be used with a group of children who share a specific learning need such as learning about story structure, drafting or remembering how to spell and recognise frequently used words. Rules about how to make a contribution may need to be established so that children listen to and develop each other's ideas. Shared writing is particularly suited to the class teaching requirements of the literacy hour since it teaches children about writing and reading and, if it is used to produce a large class book, this can be used for shared reading. Children remember and delight in reading the texts they have composed.

The activity usually begins with the teacher and children discussing the topic for the writing. If the activity is new to the class it may be best to use shared writing to retell a familiar story, write a letter, produce an account of a visit, make a sign to go with a display or compose a poem, as these have a clear structure that can be followed by the children. It is important to be clear about the aims and purposes of the writing and make them explicit to the class as these will affect the style and content and guide the children's contributions. After the initial discussion the teacher takes the pupils through all the processes of writing as she scribes for the pupils. The first stage is to brainstorm ideas to be included in the writing. As the children contribute their ideas the teacher records these as a list or diagram. After collecting the ideas on content the group consider which ideas should come at the beginning, middle and end of the writing. The teacher then numbers the ideas in the order they will occur in the text to form a plan. Working from the plan, the children and the teacher begin to compose the writing. The initial ideas are reworked, words are changed and sentences are composed as the group focus on the writing. At the end of this stage the first draft of the writing, probably containing false starts and crossing out, is complete. The first draft is read through and may be revised or edited before the final draft is produced by the teacher or the children.

The completed writing may be copied out by the children to form individual letters or books they can illustrate. With a long piece individual children may copy out one section of the text to form the writing for one page of a class book. They can then illustrate their page. Alternatively the teacher may write the final draft in a large class-made book and the children's role is to provide the illustrations. This can be used for shared reading. Sometimes the teacher may stop scribing before the final draft of the writing and the children can use the plan and the draft to compose their own individual ending to the story, poem, letter or account as a group or individual activity. Whatever the final outcome of shared writing sessions it is important that the teacher has thought about this so that children will see that investing time in reading and writing is worth while.

## Modelling writing on known texts

### *When and with whom*

Suitable at Key Stage 1 and 2. It can be used once a week or more frequently with the class or groups as a shared writing activity led by the teacher and at least once a week as an independent group activity.

### *Why*

This activity helps children to become familiar with story structure, writing stories and with the composing process. It provides children with a clear structure for their own independent writing. It can also familiarise children with the language and structure of rhymes, poems and songs.

### *How*

A familiar text is used as a framework for writing which is transcribed by the teacher or the children. A story, which may be made into a class or individual books, is created by following the structure and sequence of a published book. The characters or the objects in the story may be changed, but the language and the structures of the original text remain the same. For example the teacher might use the model provided in *Where's Spot?* (Hill, 1980) to write a book entitled *Where's Jacquie?* . . . containing sentences such as 'Is she in her office? . . . Is she in the hall? . . .'. This might be rehearsed orally or written by the teacher during shared writing and then reproduced by the children in an individual writing activity.

# Using the library

## *When and with whom*

A group activity that should take place every week with Key Stage 1 pupils. Younger children will benefit from opportunities to become familiar with the range and organisation of books in the class book area before exploring the library.

## *Why*

HMI (1996) suggested that school libraries should be a 'powerhouse' of learning about reading. Regular visits to the library give children the opportunity to talk about books and recommend good reads to each other. The resources in the library increase children's access to the wider world of books. Having access to a library and being able to find and select their own books enable children to apply their reading to their own interests and to extend their reading diet. To benefit in these ways children need to be familiar with the way in which libraries are organised.

## *How*

Children need regular opportunities to visit the library. Initially this can take place in groups with an adult. The children can browse freely at first. On later occasions their attention might be drawn to a particular type of text. Once they are familiar with some sections of the library they can be given tasks such as finding a book about a specific topic. The range of books the children collect can be discussed. Other tasks can help the children to discover more about the way books are organised. Being asked to find a book about ships may lead the children to the transport, history, geography and science sections. Book-finding tasks can also be made specific. These activities will help children to locate books that can be used for work in class or help them to explore their own interests. Children require practice and guidance as they often find it difficult to relate an item of interest to the headings used in libraries. Using libraries effectively also depends on knowledge of alphabetical order. Work on this in the class can be supplemented by practice at locating authors in the library. Teachers can devise quizzes and book trails to help. The children also need to become familiar with the procedure for borrowing and returning books to the library. Once the children understand the library system they will benefit from regular timetabled sessions which enable them to use the book collection the school has. Experience at understanding library systems can be reinforced when children use and select books from the class book area.

## Reviewing learning

### *When and with whom*

Individuals, but not every child every day, at least once a day. Plenary sessions during the literacy hour are ideal.

### *Why*

Reflecting on work is an important part of learning. It reinforces what has been learned and provides children with an opportunity to organise their knowledge and integrate it with previous experiences. It is also a valuable, focused speaking and listening opportunity. Review sessions enable teachers to give children feedback about their learning which can be related to the processes they used as well the product that emerged. They also enable teachers to make clear to children the criteria by which learning or success is evaluated. Review sessions should spread good ideas and provide an opportunity for teachers to encourage and praise pupils. They also give the teacher the opportunity to evaluate the work of groups which she has not overseen directly.

### *How*

The final part of a session devoted to reading and writing can be used for children to talk about the activities they have undertaken, explain what they have learned, justify what they did, share any problems they encountered and ask for suggestions from the class. In order that this is a positive learning experience, the teacher needs to create an atmosphere of constructive criticism for this session, so that she and the class can offer feedback that is helpful rather than counterproductive.

## Crosscurricular links

### *Why*

Books can become the starting point for further study of the text and exploration of issues and ideas they contain. The *Framework for Teaching* (DfEE, 1998) promotes a literature-based curriculum and consequently supports crosscurricular links which help children to explore books in depth and relate reading to their own lives and to real circumstances. Recreating stories through art and design technology, undertaking science activities that are related to a text, exploring history, geography and equality issues contained in a text, preparing a story for presentation to another class or for an assembly or using the book as a starting point for writing or a discussion all help children to revisit books, explore what they have read and consider how reading contributes to everyday experiences. The possibilities for crosscurricular links which start from books are endless. They can create a context in which

- concepts are considered;
- existing perspectives are challenged;
- issues are examined;
- time and place are explored;
- links between reading, speaking, listening and writing are made;
- difficult issues can be explored safely;
- children can develop empathy;
- children explore their own creativity and ability to solve problems; and
- children are led back to the main text, other texts and information books.

## *How*

Select books that deserve revisiting and merit detailed exploration when making choices about texts that are to be used for shared and group reading. Art activities that relate to the text, for example collaborative paintings of the main events in a book, can be displayed as an unfolding pictorial sequence. The children can be asked to solve a problem that has been identified in the text by, for example, making a home for Charlie in *Charlie's House* (Schermbrucker, 1992) or discovering how many animals Mr Gumpy can really take on his boat (Burningham, 1978). Collections of objects and materials related to a text can be used for counting, sorting, matching and making sets which explore number, similarities and properties. The children can be involved in making tapes of the book, story props, puppets and language games all of which could involve speaking and listening, writing, art, technology and mathematics. Making familiar stories into a play encourages exploration of language and grammar and drama sessions based on known stories can include songs and music created by the children. The children can be asked what aspect of the text they would like to investigate. For example, with *Charlie's House* (Scherm-brucker, 1992), the children may want to examine the life of children in South Africa in greater depth. Many stories for young children are arranged around a sequence of events and the passage of time and contain the potential for the exploration of historical concepts. Teachers can also respond to the children's own concerns and interests that are manifested as they share and discuss books.

## Conclusion

In this chapter a selection of varied routines has been described. Some of the routines will be used daily, others will be used less frequently. Although some indication of appropriateness and frequency has been given, teachers, acting on their personal knowledge of their class, will decide when and how often they will be employed. All practices should be suited to the teacher's learning intentions for the children and most importantly the use of routines should provide variety and avoid monotony in learning.

## Further reading

Campbell, R. (1990) *Reading Together*, Open University Press, Milton Keynes.

Campbell, R. (1995) *Reading in the Early Years Handbook*, Open University Press, Buckingham.

Campbell, R. (1996) *Literacy in Nursery Education*, Trentham Books, Stoke-on-Trent.

Edwards, V., Goodwin, P., Hunt, G., Redfern, A., Rowe, A. and Routh, C. (1996) *Practical Ways to Organise Reading*, Reading and Language Information Centre, University of Reading.

Holdaway, D. (1979) *The Foundations of Literacy*, Ashton Scholastic, Sydney, NSW.

# 6

# Wider considerations

## Introduction

Although the knowledge, understanding and classroom techniques that teachers need are the same in all schools and with all pupils, there are some issues and some children that require and benefit from additional consideration. These relate to making arrangements to accommodate individual learner differences and involving the wider community in the school's literacy programme.

This chapter will consider:

- the contribution adults outside school can make to literacy;
- the needs of bilingual pupils;
- differences in reading development related to gender; and
- catering for children who find learning to read difficult.

## Involving adults outside school in reading

### How parents support children

Most, if not all, parents casually and informally do a great deal to promote their children's literacy learning before and outside school and many provide additional and intentional support. They supply children with the foundations for reading by

- supporting their oral language development;
- providing them with models of reading
- giving them early literacy experiences through sharing books;
- helping them to understand the value and purpose of literacy;
- buying workbooks, books and taped stories;
- joining the library; and
- giving them one-to-one teaching and practice with books and games.

There is an increasing amount of evidence about the wealth of literacy activities children participate in at home. A survey undertaken by Hall *et al.* (1989) of more than 400 families showed that many parents help children with writing at home without waiting for suggestions or support from schools. The research reported by Minns (1990) gives a detailed picture of how parents of very young children spend a great deal of time sharing books with them. Weinberger's (1996) research with families and nursery children from a variety of backgrounds revealed that 58 of the 60 children she followed owned books and over 50% had between 13 and 50 at home. These findings recognise the active role parents take in their children's learning and suggest that the help that is given is widespread.

## *Why schools want to involve parents further*

The benefits of active parental interest in education at home and at school have been demonstrated in a large number of studies undertaken over the past 20 years. The initiatives which followed the *Plowden Report* (DES, 1967), such as the Haringey Reading Project (Hewison and Tizard, 1980) and the Belfield Reading Project (Jackson and Hannon, 1981), showed how direct parental involvement in reading with children raises achievement and improves motivation. More recent research has continued to show that this practice does accelerate reading success (Topping and Wolfendale, 1985).

Children benefit from schools and parents who recognise the contribution each makes to the education of young children and from both parties working together in mutually supportive ways. When parents understand what schools are doing and when teachers accept parents as educators who make a valuable contribution to children's learning, parents are more likely to support rather than resist what schools are doing. When children feel that teachers and parents have shared values and aims they are less likely to reject school or learning.

Teachers have the professional expertise to extend the scope of children's learning in imaginative and knowledgeable ways. They have a wider vision of learning and access to resources that are not available to parents. At home children can gain additional practice in reading one to one with an adult and have the opportunity to participate in the real-world application and uses of reading. They can learn about the relevance of reading in the lives of others and, by association, in their own lives. The continuity of experience between school and home helps children to experience a broad range of reading applications and gain practice at becoming literate.

When parents and teachers work together:

### Parents benefit from

- Being valued;
- understanding what schools do and why;
- knowing more about their child's learning experiences and progress; and
- being able to provide children with additional and valuable reading experiences.

### Teachers benefit from

- Finding out about children's existing learning;
- extending rather than replicating children's experiences and understanding;
- gaining additional support for their work; and
- being respected for their expertise.

### Children benefit from

- Teaching that builds on their strengths, experiences and interests;
- continuity between learning at school and home;
- support that is targeted on their needs;
- learning in both intimate and structured environments; and
- opportunities to apply their learning outside school.

The National Literacy Strategy (DfEE, 1997) recognises the learning gains that can result from teachers and parents working together and has called for systematic approaches to linking home and school to support reading. It recommends home–school contracts, regular reading homework, workshops and meetings with parents to discuss reading as mechanisms to sustain parental involvement.

## Establishing productive relationships between home and school

Beneficial home–school relationships are most likely to occur when schools have a coherent policy which is systematically implemented each year and in every class. Involving parents in children's learning requires prior consideration of the potential advantages, pitfalls, support, resources and commitment that will be involved. This can be documented in a policy which identifies the purposes of the scheme and details the activities that will be used to maintain parental interest and enable the scheme to achieve its aims. The precise nature of the events is less important than recognising that it is important to maintain the momentum and the high profile of partnership with parents.

The first contact between schools and parents usually takes place when parents visit the school before registering their child. During their initial visit to the school, parents can be given information about the school's ethos, expectations and teaching style. Other early contacts may include home visits by teachers to children's homes and meetings in school for new parents. Early meetings provide schools with the opportunity to demonstrate the value they place on the learning children bring to school. When parents are asked about their child's language abilities and interests, staff can make clear why this information is useful and how it benefits learning at school. Involving parents in this way from the start, acknowledges and values parents' intimate knowledge of their own children and signals that although once children start school there is an important professional input to their learning, the parents' contribution and knowledge are still significant.

Very often, once children have begun school, parents are given an introduction to the home–school reading arrangements. Teachers explain the role parents can play in their child's reading development and parents are supplied with written information which explains what the school does and what parents can do and gives specific examples of how to share books with children and encourage them to read. It may also contain details of special events such as bookshops, workshops, book week and poetry day. Staff may explain the practical arrangements for the home–school reading scheme such as when books are sent home, how they are returned and how to fill in the child's reading notebook. This early curriculum evening is a good forum for the exchange of information and expectations between parents and staff. However one meeting will not be able to clear up all questions, sustain interest throughout the early years or establish an enduring and productive relationship between school and home. During the initial meeting about reading parents may take away an impression of what the school does and their role but it is often when they begin to work with their child or see at first hand what their child is reading and the progress that is being made that they begin to have queries.

Many schools hold further meetings at regular intervals to sustain involvement, facilitate the transfer of information and ensure there is shared understanding about reading. Recently there have been suggestions that the format and content of such meetings could be much more flexible than a great deal of present practice (Hancock, 1995). Rather than teachers setting the agenda for what parents are expected to do about reading at home, they could use meetings with parents to begin a genuine dialogue about reading, learning and teaching. They could find out what parents already do without being prompted by the school. The research evidence (Hall *et al.*, 1989; Minns, 1990; Weinberger, 1996) suggests that this is now varied and considerable. They might then ask parents what they would like to do to support their children's literacy learning and suggest practices that are appropriate to their aims, their existing help, their skills and their knowledge. For some parents, teachers may continue to suggest they share books or play language games with children; others may need simpler and others more sophisticated advice. Some parents may need teachers to work with them to devise meaningful and effective practices that extend what already takes place at home. Parents who lack confidence may need special support in order to work with their child on reading. Simply expecting parents to do what the school asks may offend some parents who already do a great deal to help their child or could intimidate parents who themselves feel insecure about literacy. As Lochrie *et al.* (1993, p. 1) wrote: 'Partnership requires a shared sense of purpose, mutual respect, and the willingness to negotiate.'

In the National Literacy Strategy (DfEE, 1997) it is suggested that the targets that are set for children's reading and writing should be shared with parents twice a year with the expectation they will work on these with their child. These could be explained during parent interviews or special reading interviews. To ensure all parents can attend individual meetings they should be contacted personally through written invitations, conversations or phone calls. Day and evening appointments should be offered in order to suit parents' circumstances. This meeting may provide the teacher with the opportunity to clarify any queries the parents might have about reading, be used to exchange information and enable the teacher and the parent to discuss what help can provided at home.

Additional communication about reading might take place through the use of the reading diary and meetings with the parent body to discuss SATs, demonstrate new resources, show videos of children reading in school or at the beginning of a new school year. Reading diaries are often poorly used as commentaries on children's reading (Medwell, 1996). Comments such as 'lovely reading' are not helpful in understanding what the child can do, needs help with or needs to read next. Rather than being used to comment generally on the child's reading of a particular text they could be used to exchange factual information such as asking and answering questions. At times they could be used to track a child's progress towards the target for reading that both parents and teacher are working on. Book events such as a new or second-hand book shop, book week or poetry day provide further opportunities to discuss reading with parents. Children too can write notes and letters to interested adults about their reading experiences in school to keep them informed.

## Volunteers in school

Parents can be invited to contribute to the reading curriculum in school, either by coming into school to work with the children or the teacher or by producing materials at home. When parents are asked to work in school the staff can give some examples of how this can be done. They can work with groups of children on guided reading, involve themselves with role play in the imaginative play area, work with children on the computer, scribe for beginning writers, read to small groups of children or they might be able to supervise a practical activity such as model making to free the teacher to work with other children on literacy activities. Some parents may feel more comfortable working for the school at home. They too can make a contribution. There are many ways volunteers can be helpful to teachers and children at school. The following list suggests some of these:

- taking charge of the library;
- running a school book club or shop;
- talking to pupils while supervising activities;
- leading activities such as cooking which involve reading and discussion;
- teaching games, songs and rhymes to pupils;
- helping with school drama productions;
- telling and reading stories to children;
- supervising children who are reading in their mother tongue;
- helping children to use the computer;
- making books with children;
- acting as a scribe;
- listening to individual children read;
- contributing to records of their own children;
- recording songs, rhymes and stories on tape;
- writing books for children;
- translating children's writing, published books, signs, labels, notices and letters; and
- contributing to book week or poetry day.

When parents are invited to work with the school they should be provided with training by the staff. In order for teachers and parents to work together, it is important that all volunteer helpers in school are clear about what they are expected to do and that their work is carefully managed and explained by the class teacher. Involving parents in the classroom and demonstrating positive strategies which can be used at home can lead to gains in shared understanding and communication between home and school, raised levels of enthusiasm and commitment and improvements in the confidence of volunteers.

In order to be actively and productively involved in children's education, parents need information about the school's way of working, what they can do and how they can do it at school and at home. The more understanding they have the more confident they will be about participating in the life and work of the school. From the start of the child's school career parents can be given the message that education takes place at home and at school, that children's learning develops in a spirit of partnership between home and school and that it is important for both partners, parents and professionals, to be aware of children's learning experiences in and out of school. Teachers should not dominate this relationship. If they do it is no longer a partnership. They need to feel secure about their work with parents and work with them with the shared aim of developing all children's capacities as readers.

## Bilingual learners

Bilingual learners are children who speak a language other than English at home. When they start school they may have different degrees of competence in English. Some children may have a good understanding and be confident in their use of English while others may not be able to communicate in English very easily. Children who start school with more competence in a language other than English and who are developing their use and understanding of English may need additional support and special consideration in order to become confident readers.

### *Developing oral language*

Reading can help young bilingual children to learn to speak in English. It can help to develop their vocabulary and their knowledge of the structures of the language. Learning to read in English does not need to be delayed until children have acquired a degree of competence in spoken English. It should accompany oral language development. Children can learn to read before they have oral competence in a new language and reading leads to oral language development (Gregory, 1996).

Some oral language activities that are particularly appropriate for bilingual children are also useful as a means of developing the key skills of reading, as the following list indicates:

## Activities that develop phonological awareness

- Listening to and joining in with songs and rhymes;
- circle games;
- listening games; and
- 'I Spy' and other language games.

## Activities that develop word recognition

- Collaborative games involving naming and reading;
- sorting, matching and labelling activities;
- listening to, reading and rereading familiar stories.

## Activities that develop contextual understanding

- Listening to stories in English;
- joining in with telling stories activities in a group;
- imaginative play with others using literacy resources; and
- role play based on familiar stories.

# Learning to read in an additional language

For most bilingual children, literacy will be an established part of their home experience and some may be receiving instruction in the written form of their home language at a community school. The majority of bilingual learners, like their monolingual peers, will already have insights into the purposes of reading, what it means to be a reader, the way in which written text works and the connection between oral and written language and these understandings provide a means of entry into reading in English. It is important to remember this and not disregard what bilingual pupils bring to school or adopt a narrow view of literacy as the ability to read and write in English (Verma, 1984).

Bilingual learners approach learning to read and draw on similar strategies as those used by fluent English speakers. For this reason they should participate fully in the reading curriculum in the class and should be introduced to reading and to books in the way the teacher considers best for all children. However, their experience of another language system and their limited competence in English may influence the way they are able to use these strategies. The cues which British-born English-speaking pupils draw upon when reading may not be immediately accessible to them. Some developing bilinguals who have had experience with reading in their first language may need to refine their existing knowledge about reading when learning to read in English. Teachers may need to be aware of this while the children's oral fluency is developing and their experience with written English is increasing so they can provide them with appropriate help and support.

## Text-level strategies

Readers draw on their own familiarity with the beliefs, knowledge, feelings, attitudes, behaviour and events expressed in a text in order to reconstruct the author's meaning. In order to do this the reader needs to be familiar with the culture in which books are set (Halliday and Hassan, 1985). British-born English speakers usually take western cultural contexts for granted when reading and are often not aware of the difficulties this may cause to children with a different repertoire of cultural awareness and different levels of familiarity with British customs. In order to avoid problems that might be caused by unfamiliar settings and cultural assumptions teachers may need to appraise the books they offer from the standpoint of the child. For children who are new to Britain or whose lifestyle is unlikely to have brought them into contact with some of the experiences that are described in books for young children teachers might try to provide books written by bilingual authors whose experiences might match those of some bilingual learners. Alternatively they may offer them books that do not contain references to culturally specific customs.

Children's reading is supported when they use their knowledge of the world, oral language abilities, experiences with books and knowledge of the subject-matter in conjunction with the words on the page. Through listening to stories children also build up a known set of words and phrases that often appear in books and this can help them to predict sequences or individual words. Bilingual learners who may have limited experience of oral and written English will receive less support from their prior experiences than native English speakers. They may not always be familiar with the vocabulary they encounter in books and may need additional preparation and discussion before and after they read to help them to use contextual information and semantic strategies and to ensure they are understanding what is read.

## Sentence-level strategies

Bilingual learners may only have a partial understanding of the syntactic structure of the English language. For example, they may be more familiar with the subject–object–verb structure, which is used in Punjabi and Urdu, than the subject–verb–object structure commonly found in English. Their lack of familiarity with English grammar may restrict the help they receive from sentence structure to predict unknown words. They might also be unaware of the precise details of grammatical appropriate words, such as word endings that indicate tense. They might not be able to judge the grammatical correctness of their reading and this will restrict their ability to correct their mistakes. As with other inexperienced readers they will benefit from frequent opportunities to hear written language read aloud in order to become familiar with the structures of the English language.

### Word-level strategies

Readers draw on grapho-phonic information to complement the other strategies that are used when reading. With its alphabet of 26 letters representing about 44 distinct sounds and with its comparatively complex spelling patterns, English has a grapho-phonic system which can be difficult for any young child to learn and teaching all children about phonics is best delayed until they have acquired some familiarity and fluency in reading. Some bilingual learners may have additional problems with phonics that mean it is unwise to introduce this strategy too early. For example, children from Spanish-speaking backgrounds may have too great an expectation of the alphabetical consistency of written language, while those familiar with ideographic text, such as Mandarin, may initially have a very limited awareness of sound–symbol correspondences. Emphasising individual letter sounds and sound combinations when the child is just acquiring a vocabulary of common words and an awareness of pronunciation and intonation in English could be unnecessarily confusing and likely to be pointless until children understand the meaning of individual words. To be asked to analyse words into their constituent parts and remember small sounds as well as the sounds of complete words introduces a demanding abstraction that may be difficult to grasp. Children who are learning English may go through a stage when they are unable to distinguish between or use similar sounds. For example *sh* may be replaced by *s*, or *r* and *l* may be confused (Edwards, 1995). This again can make it difficult for some children to learn and apply phonics. Introducing bilingual children to the use of phonics as a support for reading is probably best done incidentally and as the child's competence at oral language and familiarity with reading increase.

A few guidelines will help teachers to support children who are learning to read in English as an additional language. These include:

- recognising and valuing children's knowledge of other languages;
- finding out about the child's previous reading experiences;
- using materials that match the children's experience and understanding;
- providing a rich and exciting reading environment;

- emphasising reading for meaning and enjoyment; and
- providing dual and home language texts to develop awareness of written language.

Teachers may also be able to provide children with support that compensates for their lack of experience with English texts during individual reading sessions. They can prepare children for sharing an unfamiliar text by discussing the title and the cover and helping the child to understand what the book might be about. The teacher and the child might look through the whole book and focus on the illustrations to get a sense of the contents. Key words and unfamiliar phrases can be isolated and discussed. The adult might read the text and invite the child to observe the text as she reads. If the text is reread the child can be invited to join in if he or she has sufficient experience to do this. The teacher can also model how to retell stories by using the illustrations. Discussions and reading with children familiarise them with language structures and books and over time will give children the experience and confidence they need to begin to read independently.

## Activities to develop reading

There is no evidence to suggest that specially designed language and reading programmes are more effective than the best of good practice when teaching young bilingual learners to read (Merchant, 1992). The book-based curriculum outlined in the *Framework for Teaching* (DfEE, 1998) is an ideal way of introducing bilingual children to reading as many writers have suggested (Hester, 1983; Ellis and Barrs, 1996). Listening to stories at story times and during shared reading sessions familiarises children with word order, vocabulary and pronunciation for oral language development and at the same time introduces children to the visual aspect of letters and words and the structures of the language that are important for reading. Sharing books is a productive starting point for developing reading with bilingual children as texts provide visual support for understanding. As they are returned to and reread children become familiar with the text and gradually they feel sufficiently confident to read known stories with others or alone.

During the literacy hour children are expected to work on activities related to texts that have been introduced during shared reading. If teachers consider the needs of bilingual learners and the stage they have reached in their understanding of spoken and written English they will be able to design activities bilingual children can complete successfully. Providing opportunities to work with others who model responses, designing activities that encourage exploration and reading of books, providing visual support and limiting written tasks will help to make group activities a productive time for bilingual learners.

Group work is particularly important for children who are learning English. The practical nature of group work generally presents children with contextual support which helps them to understand what they are required to do. Working with English-speaking children provides bilingual learners with an important opportunity to learn English, as the English speakers in the group provide language models and act as role models for participation. Children want to interact with others and to do this they need to share a common language so, when they are working in groups with children who are using English, they will need, want and begin to develop a language that enables them to participate fully in the group. They will be encouraged to use language for expressing their understanding of activities they are involved in as well as for listening and responding to the contributions of others. Collaborative work plays an important part in helping the development of oral language and supports reading development if combined with book-based activities.

Thinking about the composition of the group will contribute to the learning that ensues. It may be helpful to include bilingual learners in groups with sociable and helpful children or those with compatible personalities. Sometimes groups can consist of children who share the same first language, particularly if bilingual support is available. The teacher may also need to consider which groups are supported by her or other adults. As with all collaborative work successful outcomes are more likely to result when tasks are introduced and explained clearly before the children begin their work.

Some suggestions for activities that could be given to bilingual and other beginning readers follow:

- listening to and reading taped stories;
- using story visuals in the listening area;
- making and labelling models arising from the story;
- making and labelling collections of items related to the book;
- recreating the sequence of the text using pictures;
- using a set of sequencing cards to retell stories;
- making and playing a bingo game based on the story;
- listening to a story while following an illustrated and simply labelled story map;
- making puppets of the characters in the story;
- making story visuals to retell the story;
- making a dual language version of a familiar book;
- creating a new ending for a known story;
- making a book based on a familiar book;

- following up one aspect of the story through crosscurricular activities;
- watching story videos;
- making simple books containing repetitive language structures;
- making alphabet and counting books, possibly in two languages; and
- making posters connected to books.

In addition, reading with an adult, shared reading, paired reading with a reading partner, participating in guided group reading and shared writing sessions present further opportunities for learning to read.

It is also important to encourage the parents of bilingual children to share books with children at home. Although they may not speak or read English fluently, parents will be able to listen to the child reading a book, offer encouragement and discuss the book using the pictures as a prompt. They will also be able to tell or read stories to children in their first language. If this is not possible older siblings might be able to read with children or they could be given taped stories or reading games to play at home. Teachers will want to find ways of making sure bilingual children are provided with opportunities to become familiar with books and practise reading both in and out of school.

## *Books for the multilingual classroom*

Besides developing children's language and reading, stories provide children with personal and emotional experiences that are important for their social development and for their learning in its widest sense. This means that books need to be selected with attention to the depth of their content and their ability to offer enriching experiences to children. For inexperienced readers stories need to be simple enough to allow access – culturally appropriate and of a high enough quality to remain interesting even after being read many times. Bilingual learners also benefit from access to stories in the language they understand most easily. If possible story sessions, taped stories in home languages and dual language texts should be provided in addition to resources in English.

Bilingual learners, just like fluent English speakers, benefit from reading and using real books rather than reading scheme books. In general the range, diversity and relevance of picture books are much greater than those available in scheme books. They are more likely to contain natural oral language patterns and encourage the development of a wide range of reading strategies. Some good-quality story books are also available in dual language versions. By carefully selecting books the reading curriculum can be resourced with books that are rich enough to be told and listened to frequently and to be explored in detail. The following criteria may be helpful when selecting books for bilingual learners.

As far as possible the books should

- contain positive images of all children;
- tell an interesting and worthwhile story;
- be predictable;
- contain repeated sequences of words;
- be easy for children to retell;
- have illustrations that support the understanding of the text;
- contain familiar events and characters children can identify with;
- use simple grammatical patterns and an accessible vocabulary; and
- provide models for the children's own writing.

Caption books, wordless picture books, rhyming texts as well as stories and information books also provide opportunities for children to learn about the strategies and cues used when reading.

## Gender and reading

From the earliest stages of education until they leave school girls seem to find books and reading more interesting than boys. Girls happily discuss books and recommend titles to each other while boys rarely exchange books or information about books with friends (QCA, 1997). In the main girls learn to read more quickly, with more ease and with greater success than boys. Boys tend to read less from choice and read a narrower range of books than girls. For example they are often reluctant to read poetry and fiction that raises issues or examines experiences, preferring instead a diet of non-fiction texts or action stories. Boys lag behind girls in their reading at the primary stage and this gap widens as they get older. The majority of children with literacy problems in the early years are boys and later in their school career they perform less well in language-related subjects. In GCSEs girls are one and a half times more likely to have a high grade than boys and are twice as likely to gain an A-level in English.

A number of possible explanations for these differences have been suggested. General expectations about the behaviour of girls and boys may mean that reading is viewed as a more suitable leisure activity for girls who tend to be quieter and more introspective than for boys who are often more energetic and physical. Girls are also expected to read and to enjoy reading. In the early years, the reading curriculum is

largely constructed around stories and, although boys may enjoy listening to stories as much as girls do, using stories as reading material
may not necessarily invite them to become readers. Girls' and boys'
reading interests and habits are affected by the models of adult
readers they see and it is known that women read more fiction than
men and that adult male readers tend to read information texts, often
linked to their work or their hobbies. If boys do not see men reading
fiction this may influence their interest in a story-based reading curriculum. A study undertaken in nursery classes and nurseries (Hodgeon,
1984) found that girls' interest and ability in reading is supported by
the predominantly female culture of early years settings. The girls in
the nurseries spent more time near their teachers and as a result had
more access to stories and literacy activities and gained greater experience of reading and books than the boys.

The polarity of adult reading habits and the emphasis on story in
the early years have disadvantages for girls as well as boys. For both
sexes, much of their learning in their later school careers will depend a
great deal on their ability to read a wide range of texts and to use
information material successfully. Both boys and girls could benefit
from an earlier introduction and greater use of information texts as
they learn to read. The differences in attitudes and success at reading
manifested by boys and girls seem to be linked to a number of cultural
and societal expectations and norms which are beyond the control of
the teacher. However, whatever the external causes for the differences
in attitudes and achievement in reading, there is good reason to consider making some changes to some aspects of the reading curriculum
in order to prevent some boys from failing and to encourage more
girls to use their reading to support their learning.

## *Resources*

One of the easiest areas of the curriculum to examine and change are
the books provided for children. Paying careful attention to the images and messages contained in books is not a new idea. More than 20
years ago articles and books were appearing about sexism in children's literature (Lobban, 1975; Zimet, 1976). Although gender and
books has continued to receive a trickle of attention it is perhaps time
to re-examine the resources we provide for children in order to try to
turn around boy's underachievement and widen the range of reading
girls and boys undertake.

Whilst attitudes about male and female behaviour may be formed
and reinforced outside school, children today are able to question
stereotypical assumptions. Ridley (1995) describes a group of year-4

pupils who had a shrewd awareness of gender issues and knew that society expected boys and girls to behave in certain ways. If teachers can build on children's existing understanding by helping them to question the rightness of what they know exists and offer alternative ways of behaving to both sexes this might help to extend children's perceptions of appropriate reading behaviours.

The texts offered to children and the teaching that accompanies the examination of texts might play a part in extending children's involvement and interest in reading. All texts carry values which can unconsciously affect readers. While it is right that more books now show girls and women in more active roles, this may also reinforce boys' beliefs that energetic pursuits rather than quiet activities are important. Catering for boys' reading tastes by providing them with comic and adventure books may also contribute to this. A diet of reading material that validates action and sensation and pays little attention to reflection may help to reinforce their assumption that reading is not for them. It will do little to persuade them that quiet concentration, which is what is required for reading, has a place in their lives.

To be fair to both girls and boys and to persuade both sexes to read more widely and to regard reading as a high-status activity books need to be selected with care. There is a need for books that portray females realistically in everyday situations. Female qualities and characters need to be seen as valuable in their own right not only when they are portrayed as adventurous or dominant. Books containing male characters who do not always have adventures or perform heroic deeds and that show boys and men who are sometimes caring, sad or afraid would provide models of more thoughtful behaviour. Both boys and girls need to learn that reading is an acceptable and interesting pursuit for both sexes. Thinking about how the books we provide might help them to realise this could be an important step on the way.

## Practical strategies to foster a gender-fair reading curriculum

Carefully selecting the resources available for children will not be sufficient to change children's attitudes, forestall boy's disenchantment with reading or automatically lead girls to information books. Teachers will also need to take some practical measures to enhance the achievement of boys and girls. Some strategies teachers may consider using are given in the list that follows:

- ensure information books are included in the reading area in the classroom;

- teach children how to read and use information books;
- help children select information books that are related to their interests;
- include non-fiction in the reading curriculum from the earliest stages;
- organise group reading in single-sex groups when reading poetry or non-fiction;
- keep records of the books children read and monitor their selection;
- provide children with books that extend their choices;
- use and display books which contain images of boys and men as readers;
- involve older boys, male teachers, fathers and male visitors in reading activities;
- invite male story tellers to school;
- create play areas where male and female workers use reading equally;
- use ICT as a resource for reading;
- encourage boys to participate in quieter classroom activities;
- provide opportunities for reading and language in more physical and outdoor activities;
- give children a purposeful and tangible outcome for their reading;
- ensure assessment covers the reading and use of non-fiction as well as fiction;
- address gender issues with parents; and
- make positive efforts to involve male carers in the home–school reading programme.

## Children who find learning to read difficult

Children who do not make good progress in reading take up a great deal of teachers' attention and cause them a great deal of concern. Teachers are very aware of the damaging consequences of being unable to read. They know that children who find reading a struggle often have poor self-esteem and manifest problem behaviours in school. They also recognise that in the world beyond school, illiteracy limits personal independence and access to many potentially rewarding experiences and can make it difficult to fulfil the daily requirements of living in the twentieth century.

### *Identifying difficulties*

Before thinking about specific ways of supporting children who are experiencing difficulties, teachers need to analyse the sort of difficulty the child has and think about its cause. This will help them to focus their teaching and address the particular problems each child has. Usually we notice reading difficulties because children

- are unable to read more than a few words without help;
- do not understand what they read;
- do not want to read;
- think they cannot read; and
- do not want to read the texts provided for them.

Some children may display several of these traits. If children are unable to read without support they may have difficulty understanding what they read because their reading is frequently interrupted as they struggle to identify words and wait for help. Children who find reading difficult are unlikely to enjoy reading or feel confident about their ability to read and will often try to avoid reading. Children who are poor readers will want to find excuses for their difficulties and, as a means of defending themselves, they may protest that the books they are given to read are boring and make reading difficult. Identifying the different types of reading difficulty reminds us that remediation may need to address a number of areas. These are the child's skills and strategies, attitudes and confidence and the need to provide suitable texts that are both motivating and accessible.

Before taking any action it is important to try to identify the reasons for children's difficulties. The following are often cited as the causes of or contributory factors to reading failure:

## Physical factors

- Visual impairment;
- hearing problems;
- language delay or disorder; and
- ill-health resulting in prolonged or frequent absence from school.

## Environmental factors

- High adult expectations and pressure;
- absence of books at home; and
- unfavourable home circumstances.

## School factors

- Irrelevant materials;
- teacher expectations too high;
- teacher expectations too low;

- the purposes for reading not made clear to the children;
- poorly organised reading programme; and
- teachers responding negatively to children who are slow to start reading.

### Personal characteristics

- Anxiety;
- lack of motivation;
- short attention span;
- poor self-image;
- not understanding what reading is for; and
- general learning difficulties.

The more we understand about the type of difficulty each child has and why this difficulty has arisen, the more likely we are to be able to help children overcome their problems. Knowing about the cause of the problem allows teachers to compensate for or address this and identifying the type of difficulty enables teachers to focus their teaching sharply. Any action that is then taken will be of most benefit to the child because it will be directly linked to what is wrong.

Some causes of reading difficulty may be corrected very easily. For example physical factors can often be improved by referring the child for a sight or hearing test. Physical problems do not mean the child cannot or will not ever be able to read, but that there are tangible reasons why the child is experiencing problems. Environmental difficulties may be solved or at least helped by discussions with parents and carers about their expectations for the child and their own interest in reading. Home and school may then be able to work together at helping the child to become a reader. The absence of books at home need not prevent the child from learning to read; other forms of text such as teletext, newspapers and junk mail will probably have introduced the child to print, but it may be that the teacher has to devote more time to ensuring that the child who lives in a home that has limited literacy provision gains as much experience as possible with books at school. The absence of positive role models for reading at home make it essential that the child learns about the purpose and relevance of literacy in his or her own life. Difficulties at home resulting in emotional trauma for the child such as those accompanying a separation or bereavement may be temporary and do not mean the child has a reading problem. The events in his or her life at the moment may be making it temporarily hard for the child to concentrate on learning.

## *Providing for children with difficulties*

In order to match her teaching to the needs of a child who is experiencing difficulties the teacher may want to set aside a time to analyse his or her reading by carrying out a miscue analysis. This will help her to identify which reading strategies the child makes use of and those he or she does not use. A miscue should reveal whether the child is reading for meaning, reading on or rereading when he or she encounters difficulties, self-correcting, using phonic strategies or drawing on a sight vocabulary of known words. A miscue analysis should provide a much clearer picture of where the child's strengths and weaknesses lie and help to identify where the child needs help. The results of a miscue should lead to changes to the reading activities and programme planned for children with difficulties. These should be suited to the level the child has reached and form part of a regular, systematic and structured teaching programme that has clear and realisable aims.

The following activities might be used to support children whose difficulties have arisen from not using all the strategies available to them:

### *Developing semantic and syntactic strategies*

- Reading books which have accompanying tapes;
- undertaking shared writing in small groups;
- making a picture sequence of a favourite book;
- participating in a classroom treasure hunt by finding written clues;
- reading simple plays;
- participating in group-guided reading using appropriate texts;
- reading and sharing books with a partner;
- using DEV TRAY alone or with a partner on the computer;
- undertaking cloze procedure;
- carrying out sequencing activities;
- writing personal books with the help of an adult scribe; and
- using story props to retell stories.

### *Developing a sight vocabulary*

- Making a book containing personally important words to use as a reading book and as a dictionary when writing;
- making word and picture games such as pairs, lotto or dominoes using words from familiar and popular books;
- using known books to hunt for words;
- writing out familiar rhymes and jingles for the child to read; and
- reading from a stock of familiar books that contain simple, repetitive texts.

## Developing grapho-phonic strategies

- Playing snap, matching and lotto games using single letters and rhyming words;
- talking about words after shared reading or individual reading sessions;
- encouraging the child to look at the ends and beginnings of words;
- playing oral word games such as 'I Spy';
- hunting in books for words that begin with specific letters;
- building up a repertoire of rhymes and jingles, songs and jokes; and
- reading entertaining books with simple rhyming texts.

Individual reading sessions will play a large part in helping struggling readers to overcome their difficulties. These need to be planned so that children are in a position to read as well as they can and include support and teaching that enables them to learn the reading strategies that will help them to read more effectively.

Reading sessions need to be long enough for the teacher and child to spend time discussing the text both before and after the reading. The book read might be selected by the child from one of the many books that have been introduced to the class during shared reading or at story times. The child may have also explored the book independently by listening to a taped version, using associated story props or taking it home. This familiarity with the text will help the child to read the book with more success and confidence. Before the child begins to read with the adult he or she should be given time to prepare for reading and an opportunity to talk about what the book might be about and what will happen in the story. The teacher may pose some questions about the text before the book is read to help the child to concentrate on the text. During the reading the teacher might encourage the child to guess unknown words using the context or provide words so that the reading is not interrupted. After the book has been read the teacher and the child can talk about what has been read. The teacher can then provide the child with teaching about words, letters, sounds and letter strings using the book that has been shared. Such teaching should be related to the child's needs as they were revealed during the reading session.

## Confidence and attitudes

Learning to be literate is central to the lives of most young children. All children expect to learn to read when they start school. They see that success at reading is praised by adults in and out of school and know that it is a highly regarded activity. When they have difficulty with reading they may feel that not only are they failing at reading but also that they are failing as a person. Failure at reading is very public. Children who are poor at reading are known to be so by all the members of the class, their families and their teacher. In order to avoid demonstrating their failure, children who have difficulty reading often try to avoid reading. This means they gain fewer reading experiences and accumulate less knowledge about reading than their more competent peers. This causes them to fall further behind. As they continue to experience difficulties they become anxious about reading, do not see themselves as readers and their self-confidence falters. When they do have to read they may begin to withdraw, not concentrate and appear unmotivated. Children who are distracted, expect to fail and refuse to take chances are very hard to teach and find it very hard to learn.

To help children who have lost confidence in their ability to learn to read the teacher needs to find ways of restoring their self-esteem, alleviating their fears and reducing the pressure so that they will want to learn and feel secure enough to be able to take the risks learning involves. For some children enhancing their self-esteem may be sufficient to enable them to succeed at reading. As Asher (1980) suggested, failure to learn to read often occurs not because children lack the physical or cognitive resources to succeed, but because they lose impetus and belief in themselves.

Children with low self-esteem need to be convinced they are important and that what they think and feel are valued. They can be helped to believe in themselves by adults who listen to them, provide opportunities for them to succeed and give them some control over their own learning. They need sympathetic and encouraging guidance and opportunities to practise so they can become more successful. The following strategies might be useful to teachers who are working with children with low self-esteem:

- think about the learning experiences that are offered from the child's perspective;
- acknowledge and accept the child's anger and irritation;
- organise activities which facilitate rather than impede success;
- create a classroom environment where risk taking is possible and valued;
- value the process of learning, not just the product;
- build up the child's trust by being fair, straightforward and honest;
- praise and encourage the child whenever the opportunity arises, making the reasons for your praise clear;
- set clear and achievable goals with and for the child;
- use language positively. Rather than saying, 'You aren't trying' say, 'I don't think that that is too hard for you, I think that you can do it';

- don't label struggling children as 'problems' but think of them as inexperienced;
- listen to and take seriously what children say about reading and books;
- provide books that children with low self-esteem can identify with;
- write an 'I Can . . .' book with individual children to demonstrate what they can do; and
- provide a wide variety of books at a simple level.

While some children may have developed negative attitudes towards reading because they know they are failing there may be another cause for their negativity. Some children may not realise what reading is for or what it can do. They may never have recognised or seen the point of reading or found any reward in the written word. Because they do not understand the relevance of reading they might have very little interest in becoming a reader.

If the teaching programme is not helping children to learn about the purposes of reading it may need to be changed so that the importance and relevance of reading are clear. Children learn about reading from the demonstrations of reading they see and the explanations they are given about it. Activities that trivialise reading or concentrate on learning discrete skills such as reading repetitive reading material or completing worksheets do not make the purposes for reading clear to children and might not convince them that becoming literate is a worthwhile pursuit. Reading programmes should include meaningful, intrinsically interesting activities and use materials that are motivating and linked to children's experiences and interests.

The following list suggests some ideas that can be used with children who need to be convinced about the merits of learning to read:

- demonstrate the purposes of reading print through displays of print, pupil noticeboards and reading a variety of material in the classroom;
- collect and use written material from books and magazines related to children's interests;
- let children choose their own reading material;
- match books to the child's reading ability and interests;
- follow up silent reading times with a short discussion of books children have enjoyed;
- write simple books for individual children based on their interests or with the child as the central character;
- use books composed by children as reading books;
- write letters to children which they will read;
- provide plenty of opportunities for listening to stories and information books; and

- make reading and reading activities enjoyable and give the child praise for effort and concentration.

## *Designing individual programmes*

None of the suggestions in this section are radically different from those that have appeared elsewhere in this book. Good teaching and the way in which reading is learned are the same for all learners. All children with difficulties do not necessarily need or benefit from an intensive diet of phonics or special reading books. Each child needs help that is matched to his or her particular difficulties. This can be provided through regular, systematic and sustained reading sessions and reading activities which cater for the weaknesses that have been identified:

> There is no special mystique or methodology for pupils who have difficulties with reading. Time and effort spent with such pupils are the only factors likely to be repaid with increased interest and competence. Thus we can help best by diagnosing children's differing needs in reading and by adapting *the strategies we normally use* to meet them.
>
> (Wade and Moore, 1987, p. 95)

## *Successful reading*

The intention when working with children who have found learning to read difficult is to help them to become successful readers. What counts as success will be different for every child and may be linked as much to a positive attitude towards reading as to successful performance. The child who is interested in becoming a reader and who feels he or she is a reader will make progress when his or her interest and efforts are supported. But in the long term we want all children to be able to

- make meaning from written texts;
- read with intelligence, enjoyment and economy;
- turn to books for information and enjoyment;
- know how to select books for their own purposes;
- use their knowledge of language and of the world when reading; and
- use reading strategies that, with further practice and experience, will enable them to become competent, independent and self-motivated readers.

# Conclusion

All the issues explored in this chapter will affect the way the reading curriculum is planned and implemented in school. Catering for every child's needs, whatever his or her experience and level of expertise, calls for the teacher to be flexible and sensitive to children as individuals. Effective teaching also necessitates careful monitoring of children's development and an ability to offer a broad range of learning experiences within a carefully planned reading programme.

# Further reading

Edwards, V. (1995) *Reading in Multilingual Classrooms*, Reading and Language Information Centre, University of Reading.

Gregory, E. (1996) *Making Sense of a New World*, Paul Chapman Publishing, London.

SCAA (1996) *Boys and English*, SCAA, London.

Smith, J. and Alcock, A. (1990) *Revisiting Literacy*, Open University Press, Milton Keynes.

Stacey, M. (1991) *Parents and Teachers Together*, Open University Press, Milton Keynes.

# 7

# Assessing reading

## Introduction

Assessment is an important part of teaching. It 'lies at the heart' of promoting children's learning (DES, 1988) and is 'an integral part of teaching and learning' (SCAA, 1995a). It is the process of establishing whether or not pupils have learned what was intended. Undertaking assessments can help teachers to understand what children can do and what they find difficult. Knowing this gives teachers the information they need to provide the learning opportunities and teaching that match children's needs. If teachers do not know what children know and understand they cannot teach effectively.

It is essential that assessment is undertaken with a positive appreciation of what children can do. When children are learning to speak adults reward their developing competence and accept their mistakes. They do not focus on errors and deficiencies. Acknowledging the positive does not prevent children from learning to speak; rather, it creates a climate in which children can and do learn. By looking for areas to develop it is easy to identify what children do not know and to overlook their achievements. Although the intention might be positive the effect on learners can be destructive.

The intention of this chapter is to help readers to

- view assessment as a positive activity;
- understand the principles of assessment;
- plan for assessment using a range of methods;
- use the results of assessment to inform teaching; and
- undertake the statutory assessment requirements.

## Assessment

Assessment includes all the ways of establishing what children know and can do. It consists of collecting and analysing information and evidence

131

about children's achievements and experiences by examining the processes and products of learning. Assessment of pupil learning should also be used to evaluate the appropriateness of the curriculum that is being provided. As assessment provides teachers with insights into pupil learning and into their own teaching there should be very close links between assessment and provision. In some cases classroom practices may need to be changed to ensure pupils learn what the teacher intends.

Assessment can be formative or summative. Formative assessment occurs continuously throughout a period of learning and generates information the teacher can use immediately. Summative assessment records the achievements of pupils after the completion of a phase of learning, such as at the age of 5 or at the end of a key stage. In order to make accurate judgements about children at the end of a period of learning the teacher needs to consider the range of evidence that has been collected through formative assessments during the whole phase as well as the results of tests undertaken towards the end. The information from summative assessments is usually passed on to and used by others including the child's next teacher. Both formative and summative assessment are important since in both cases the outcomes are used to inform planning and teaching and to accommodate the learning needs of pupils.

Although the principal function of assessment is to improve learners' existing abilities there are a number of other purposes for undertaking assessments, all of which are relevant to reading. It can help teachers to

- understand children's learning;
- keep track of children's progress and development;
- evaluate teaching and curriculum provision;
- inform curriculum planning;
- inform organisational choices;
- improve the quality of pupil learning;
- teach children what they need to know;
- contribute to a record of progress;
- provide a statement of current attainment;
- measure progress;
- identify or confirm difficulties;
- provide information for others; and
- demonstrate accountability to interested parties.

## Assessing reading

Assessment should enable teachers to build up a detailed account of children' strengths and weaknesses as readers. It should be used to monitor their developing knowledge, understanding, skills and attitudes (OFSTED, 1993). Knowledge about reading includes knowing

- what reading is for;
- about the use and construction of texts;
- about print and words; and
- the terminology used to discuss reading.

Understanding takes knowledge further and enables learners to put their knowledge to use. In reading children need to understand they can

- apply reading in different circumstances;
- use and evaluate what they read; and
- draw on their experience as oral language users when reading.

Knowledge and understanding provide children with information about how and when to use each of the key skills of reading. For example making decisions about when to employ phonic skills and how to use these in conjunction with other skills depend on children's understanding of the links between oral and written language and knowledge of words and texts.

Attitudes to reading and books largely determine how much practice the reader gets and what is read. Teachers will want to see children developing positive traits such as motivation, interest, confidence, concentration and effort and will act swiftly if they see children who are becoming disheartened or frustrated.

Monitoring knowledge, understanding, skills and attitudes provide the basis for the teacher's formative and summative assessment of reading. This usefully extends the information provided by externally devised tests which generally do not measure attitudes or the depth of children's understanding or knowledge. These attributes should not be neglected as they contribute to children's developing competence and may make a difference to whether children use reading for their own purposes in the world beyond the classroom and in later life.

## Formative assessment

Formative assessment can refer to the frequent and informal attention teachers give to children's reading as well as regular, planned assessment opportunities. Each time children read a piece of text or use books in the classroom the teacher is alerted to what they are able to read. Every encounter children have with texts can be a fruitful source of evidence about their reading ability. Comments from parents, other adults in school and the children all add to the teacher's picture of each child as a reader. The information gathered helps teachers to diagnose problems and to identify areas that need more attention. It provides teachers with insights into the suitability of their own practice for the needs of the children in the class.

Although children's reading development is regularly monitored, assessment involves more than noticing that children are or are not making progress. It needs to cover all aspects of reading behaviour and needs to provide teachers with detailed information. Planned and clearly focused formative assessment opportunities help teachers to

- use their time effectively;
- concentrate on specific aspects of reading development;
- ensure all aspects of reading are covered;
- ensure all children are monitored;
- gather information from a range of situations;
- make accurate judgements about strengths and weaknesses;
- collect information that can be used to plan teaching for groups rather than individuals; and
- feel in control rather than overwhelmed by assessment.

Assessment opportunities should be built into the reading curriculum and identified when weekly and half-termly plans are being prepared. Over time planned assessments should cover different aspects of reading. Although assessment opportunities are planned for and identified they do not need to be specially designed. Assessment should take place during authentic literacy activities and does not need to interrupt the normal flow of reading activities that take place. Assessment information can be gathered through observation of groups or individuals as they read, and through questioning children in teacher-led discussions, reading conferences and interviews. Teachers may decide to observe one reading activity that will be undertaken by all the children over the course of a few days. Alternatively the teacher may identify one or two children to interview each day until all the class have been assessed. The method selected will depend on what the teacher wishes to discover. Information about reading behaviour should be recorded and may include references to the Desirable Learning Outcomes and the National Curriculum level descriptions. This can provide useful information for the teacher when she is compiling the end-of-year summaries and reports for the children's next teacher and parents. In the next part of this chapter different ways of undertaking planned formative assessments that can be incorporated into established classroom routines are explained.

## Reading conferences

Although reading conferences, when children and adults share books together, are a time for developing reading they also reveal a great deal about the child's strengths and weaknesses as a reader. Their frequency and regularity mean they are probably the most common method of assessing pupils' reading. When teachers and children discuss and share books the teacher can discover a great deal of information about the aspects of reading behaviour she wishes to monitor. Teachers usually keep a record of these reading sessions in a notebook or file, allocating a number of pages for each child at the start of the year. Records such as this present a very full picture of children's reading strengths and needs when kept for some time. The example which follows is of Kerry, a 5-year-old beginning reader in a reception class. It shows how the books Kerry has read have been listed and notes made about her reading strategies and attitude to reading. It also contains notes about the support the teacher has given to Kerry based on her particular reading abilities:

**Name** Kerry   **d.o.b.** 8.10.91

| Date | Book | Child's strengths | Teacher strategies |
|------|------|-------------------|--------------------|
| 13.11.96 | *Each Peach Pear Plum* | Remembered this well. Was able to read the repeated words easily. | Discussed and found rhyming words. K is taking the book and tape home. |
| 19.11.96 | *Mr Gumpy's Outing* | K really enjoyed the language. Shows a real interest in words. Now beginning to remember words such as *can, I, you.* Enjoyed and understood the story. | Discussed and examined goat, boat, etc. Gave K *Mr Gumpy's Motor Car* to read. |

Conference records for more experienced readers might refer to specific miscues and fluency. Children who are able to read silently may select a short extract from their current book to read aloud during a conference and the teacher's assessment will take place during the discussion that follows the reading. She will also monitor the range and difficulty level of the books the child is reading. Records often reveal very positive accounts of progress and provide evidence teachers can use when writing records and reports.

## Reading interviews

Each child should have at least one reading interview with the teacher each term. In many cases this will be combined with a discussion about writing and take place within a literacy interview. The child can prepare for the session by reviewing his or her own reading diary, looking back at the list of books he or she has read and selecting a book or part of a book to read to the teacher. During the interview the child should be invited to talk about him or herself as a reader and the books he or she enjoys. As the child speaks the teacher may make notes of what is said. The child's comments may provide additional evidence for assessment and information for future planning. The child can then read the prepared text to the teacher and discuss this with her. At the end of the session the teacher and the child should agree on a target for improvement. The notes and the target should be read to the child, who can be asked whether anything needs to be changed or added. The target needs to be clear to the teacher, the child and to parents who can be given a copy. Between each interview the teacher should monitor the child's progress towards meeting the target and record any significant steps. The target can be used as the starting point for the next interview. Notes from reading interviews can be used to discuss reading with parents who may be able to support their child's improvement through activities or practice at home. This way of monitoring children's knowledge, understanding, skills, attitudes and interests can begin in the nursery. Encouraging children to reflect on their reading can help them to think more deliberately about what they are doing and where they are going. Involving children in assessments through self-evaluation enables them to make a real contribution to assessing and monitoring their own progress.

## Checklists

Checklists for reading can help teachers to keep track of what children can do. They can also be included in children's records. Checklists can take the form of a preprinted list of common reading behaviours seen as reading develops or objectives that have been achieved. Lists of behaviours are more useful than skills for nursery and reception classes as these tend to emerge first and knowledge, understanding and attitudes underpin skill development. As children demonstrate the strategies identified on the checklist, the relevant box is marked. Some teachers make one mark when the child is beginning to use a strategy and a different sort of mark when the strategy is being used confidently and consistently. This can be a useful way of showing what each child can do easily or where more practice is needed.

## *Observing reading*

When teachers make observations about children's work and progress in the course of daily classroom activities they can gain insights into the strategies children are using and their learning styles. They may also see spontaneous and important moments of literacy learning which represent a significant step in the learning development of a particular child.

Sometimes observations are preplanned and may have a specific focus, or they may occur almost incidentally. Planned observations are a particularly important assessment tool in the nursery where other assessment methods may be less appropriate. Recording observations can contribute to the picture of the child's development as a reader and help teachers to appreciate progress over time. When a number of people work with the child it is useful to discuss observations with colleagues. This is useful as individual observations can be placed in a wider context and the information they reveal can be acted on by all the staff. Some teachers find it helpful to use a loose-leaf notebook as an observation diary. Several pages in the notebook can be allocated to each child in the class. As the pages are completed they can be removed, analysed and placed in the child's record folder. One or two observations for each pupil should be made each term.

The following situations may be particularly revealing when making observations about reading. When children are

- listening to or participating in stories in sessions led by an adult;
- reading and listening to stories in the listening area;
- using story props alone or with other children;
- browsing and choosing books to read for pleasure or use;
- reading alone or with other children during shared or group reading sessions;
- reading silently during quiet reading times;
- reading voluntarily;
- using and noticing print in the classroom;
- discussing books; and
- referring to books and stories in their play

then observing children in these situations helps the teacher to build up a fuller picture of

- how the child reads – with independence, with confidence, with interest, out of choice, in English, in another language;
- when the child reads – with others, alone, out of choice; and
- what the child reads – published stories, books written by the class, information texts, dual language texts.

Observation may also provide information about some of the child's reading and book-selection strategies.

Anything that is particularly striking or that reveals a pattern in the child's behaviour should be noted and added to the reading record. The teacher may wish to follow up what has been noticed through further observation, discussion with the child or teaching. For example if a child is observed having problems when using a maths activity card the problem might be the mathematics, the terminology or reading the card. Talking to the child could identify the source of the problem and the teacher can then provide the appropriate support.

## Miscue analysis

A miscue is a deviation from the text. When children are reading they can sometimes produce words that are not those represented by the symbols they are reading. These responses are known as miscues. The word 'miscue' is used rather than mistake or error because some substitutions are appropriate and resemble the substitutions fluent readers frequently produce especially when reading at speed. All miscues reveal the reading strategies the child can use. Even if these are inappropriate, they indicate what children do know about reading. Recording and analysing miscues using the procedure suggested by Goodman and Burke (1972) is a very detailed and systematic way of listening to a child read. It is a diagnostic assessment technique which can provide the administrator with insights about the reader and the whole reading process. The information it yields is analysed carefully and is used to plan future teaching for the child. Miscue analysis requires no special materials. The child reads a book or a passage of text containing about 150 words, less if the child is very young or inexperienced. The text should not be too easy or too familiar since the miscues the child makes provide the listener with valuable information about his or her reading. But neither is it necessary to make the reading frustrating or unnecessarily difficult. The teacher requires a photocopy of the text which the child will read on which to note the

| Miscue | Symbol | Example |
|--------|--------|---------|
| Substitution | Cross out the word in the text and write in the substituted word | in the ~~corner~~ cannon |
| Non-response | Underline with dots | moor |
| Insertion | Write in the additions the child makes | In the ʌ wood  dark |
| Omission | Circle the word/s omitted | Across the passage (there) was |
| Hesitation | Insert a stroke when the child pauses for longer than is appropriate | there was a dark, dark / pussy |
| Repetition | Underline the repeated word | In the hall there |
| Reversal | Indicate with a curved line | shoes ⌣ and socks |
| Self correction | Write in the miscue, then amend with a tick | ~~Once~~ One ✓ |

**Figure 7.1**   Miscues and the symbols to represent them

miscues, although some teachers prefer to tape record the child's reading and fill in the miscues later. Before beginning the miscue analysis the teacher and child may discuss the book and the teacher may support the child as he or she reads the opening few sentences. The child will have been told that for most of this reading session the teacher will not provide the usual support and will only intervene if the child is really stuck. Once the child begins reading alone the teacher notes the miscues that occur using a consistent form of notation. Typical miscues and the symbols used to represent them are shown in Figure 7.1. The possible causes of the different types of miscue are summarised in Table 7.1.

In addition to noting the reader's miscues the teacher also observes the way in which the child reads, listening for the child's use of intonation, fluency and awareness of punctuation. After the child has finished the reading the teacher may ask the child to retell the story and ask about his or her response to what has been read. The analysis of the miscues, the teacher's observations and the child's summary and comments provide the adult with a full picture of the child's strengths and weaknesses as a reader. They indicate the strategies the child employs and his or her understanding of reading as an activity. After the analysis the teacher is then in a position to draw up an appropriate reading programme for the child. The example in Figure

**Table 7.1**  Possible causes of miscue

| Miscue | Indicates |
| --- | --- |
| Substitution | If acceptable, e.g. 'steps' for 'stairs', generally indicates that the child is understanding what is read. Fluent readers make substitutions when they are reading quickly and their eyes are ahead of their voice |
| | If unacceptable, e.g. 'forest' for 'front', the child is not understanding what is read |
| | Examine other strategies, e.g. use of initial letters, phonic and graphic cues. May be over-relying on strategies other than meaning |
| Non-response | Word or concept outside the child's experience |
| | Child lacks confidence in making predictions |
| Insertion | Fluent reading, eyes ahead of voice |
| Omission | Fluent reading, when there is no interruption to meaning. Negative omission occurs when the reader does not recognise the word |
| Hesitation | Trying to decode the text |
| | Trying to understand confusing syntax, style or meaning |
| Repetition | Uncertainty about the word or meaning |
| | Trying to understand confusing syntax, style or meaning |
| Reversal | May indicate fluent reading, where the reader is adapting what is written into a form closer to a known speech patterns, e.g. 'Martin said' rather than 'said Martin' |
| Self-correction | Understands that reading involves making meaning. Trying to make sense of the text. |

7.2, taken from Browne (1996), demonstrates a miscue analysis undertaken with Michael, aged 5, reading *A Dark, Dark Tale* (Brown, 1981).

### Analysis of Michael's reading
Michael uses grapho-phonic cues, relying a great deal on initial single letters at the beginning of words, for example when he substitutes *forest* for *front*, and *cannon* for *corner*. Sometimes he looks beyond the initial letter and uses letter strings as with *cup* for *cupboard*, *hill* for *hall* and *Ac*, *Act* and *As* for *Across*.

Some of Michael's miscues are syntactically appropriate, indicating that he understands how language works, for example *hill* for *hall*. His awareness of book language can be seen when he self-corrects the opening word and when he inserts *dark* in line 5.

| Actual Text | Michael's Reading |
|---|---|
| | One ✓ |
| 1 Once upon a time there | ~~Once~~ upon a time there |
| 2 was a dark, dark moor. | was a dark, dark m̲o̲o̲r̲. |
| 3 On the moor there was | On the moor there was |
| 4 a dark, dark wood. | a dark, dark wood. |
| | dark |
| 5 In the wood there was | In the ˅wood there was |
| 6 a dark, dark house. | a dark, dark house. |
| | forest |
| 7 At the front of the house | At the ~~front~~ of the house |
| 8 there was a dark, dark door. | there was a dark, dark door. |
| 9 Behind the door there | Behind the door there |
| | hill |
| 10 was a dark, dark hall. | was a dark, dark ~~hall~~. |
| | hill |
| 11 In the hall there were | In the ~~hall~~ there were |
| | steps |
| 12 some dark, dark stairs. | some dark, dark ~~stairs~~. |
| | steps |
| 13 Up the stairs there was | Up the ~~stairs~~ there was |
| | pussy |
| 14 a dark, dark passage. | a dark, dark/~~passage~~. |

15 Across the passage there was

A͝ A͝Ė As
A̶c̶r̶o̶s̶s̶ the passage (there) was

16 a dark, dark curtain.

cat
a dark, dark c̶u̶r̶t̶a̶i̶n̶.

17 Behind the curtain was

cat
Behind the c̶u̶r̶t̶a̶i̶n̶ was

18 a dark, dark room.

a dark, dark room.

19 In the room was a dark,

In the room was a dark,

20 dark cupboard.

cup
dark c̶u̶p̶b̶o̶a̶r̶d̶.

21 In the cupboard was

cup
In the c̶u̶p̶b̶o̶a̶r̶d̶ was

22 a dark, dark corner.

cannon
a dark, dark c̶o̶r̶n̶e̶r̶.

23 In the corner was

cannon
In the c̶o̶r̶n̶e̶r̶ was

24 a dark, dark box.

a dark, dark box.

25 And in the box there

And in the box there

26 was ... A MOUSE!

was ... A MOUSE!

**Figure 7.2** A miscue analysis

He depends a great deal on the illustrations to help him read unfamiliar words. A large black cat is featured on the cover of the book and appears in many of the illustrations; this is never referred to in the text but it seems to influence some of Michael's substitutions, for example *Behind the/cat* in line 17. The cat was the main character in Michael's retelling. In some cases the illustrations are misleading and lead to inappropriate substitutions as in lines 23 and 24, *In the cannon was a dark, dark box*. The previous page had shown a toy cannon. Many of Michael's substitutions, repetitions and hesitations indicate he is trying to understand what he is reading, for example *step's* for *stairs*, line 12. He uses a combination of grapho-phonic, syntactic and picture cues to help him decode unknown words, but he does not use the narrative itself.

Michael's retelling was brief and indicated he was distracted by the cat in the illustrations. There was little sense of story in his retelling, which was rather disjointed involving him in listing individual items rather than relating a sequence of events.

### Follow-up action

Michael approaches text confidently and believes himself to be a reader. Further experience with books and stories will add to this confidence. He is able to use grapho-phonic and pictorial cues well. He needs to be encouraged to think about the sense of what he reads, to use the context of words and sentences in books and to read on to the end of a sentence to help him tackle new words. He should be encouraged to think as he reads and to self-correct if he thinks what he reads does not make sense. He would benefit from talking about his books before and after reading. Shared reading of big books, reading with tapes and group reading might also help Michael to read with more understanding.

Miscue analysis is time consuming for the teacher, but it is truly a 'window on the reading process' (Goodman and Goodman, 1977) and many teachers find miscue analysis an illuminating experience. By administering one or two miscues with average readers or children who seem to be experiencing difficulties in reading the teacher can gather a great deal of information she can use with these pupils. She will also learn a great deal about the way she is teaching reading and the strategies she is emphasising. It may be that this will lead the teacher to focus on other strategies which will be helpful to all the children she works with. Both the National Curriculum reading task at level 2 and the examination of reading samples are based on miscue analysis.

## Reading samples

Some teachers like to incorporate reading samples into their planned schedule of assessments. They could be described as a more detailed version of a reading conference or an abbreviated form of miscue analysis. They involve teachers in listening to children read in a very focused way and result in a detailed picture of the child's reading strengths and strategies (Barrs *et al.*, 1988). They usually take place once a term with each child in the class. When undertaking a reading sample children are asked to read a whole book or a substantial piece of text aloud to an adult. This can be familiar or new to the child and may be in English or, if appropriate, in the child's heritage language. During the reading the teacher makes notes on how the child approaches text, his or her confidence, independence, involvement and enjoyment. The teacher also notes how the child uses grapho-phonic, word recognition, grammatical, bibliographic and contextual reading cues, and the balance between them. With less experienced readers teachers may be particularly interested in noting the child's use of book language, ability to read illustrations, awareness of print and skills such as directionality, one-to-one correspondence and the ability to recognise some words. After the reading the child is invited to talk about the book and this gives the teacher further insights into the child's understanding and ability to evaluate text. The teacher follows up the sample taking by making notes about the experiences and support the child should be given in order to make further progress as a reader.

## Reading journals

Children can keep their own record of what they read. If this is kept in a personal reading diary there will be space for children to write comments about some of the books or authors they encounter during the year. Reading journals are very useful to teachers when they are looking for information about the range of reading children undertake and their reading habits. When they are shared with adults they can respond to the children's comments and suggest other books they might enjoy reading.

## Pupil self-assessment

Children who monitor their own learning can gain substantially from the process. By reflecting on reading, being clear about what they are expected to achieve and being aware of the targets for their own reading development children know what they are aiming for. This will help them to participate in conferences equally and to articulate what they find difficult and where they need help. It also helps children to appreciate how the support they are given is relevant to their needs. Children can be involved in assessing their development in reading in the following ways:

- talking about reading;
- identifying aspects of reading they find difficult;
- including their comments in records;
- deciding on the targets to be set during reading interviews;

- writing an end-of-term report on their own progress; and
- keeping reading diaries.

When writing reports on their own progress children can be supported by addressing a set of questions, such as:

- What can I do easily?
- What do I find difficult?
- What do I want to be able to do?
- What would help me to do this?

## Contributions from others

Whilst a great deal of assessment is carried out by the class teacher, parents, carers and other adults who work with the children may offer further perspectives on their development in reading. Parents have a unique knowledge of their children and discussions with them can provide teachers with insights into children's abilities and interests that are not always apparent in the classroom. For example, parents of bilingual children may be able to tell the teacher about the child's knowledge and understanding of languages other than English.

Parents may talk about when and what the child chooses to read outside school, book ownership and library membership or if they notice a change in the child's attitude towards reading. Discussions with parents lead to shared understandings about expectations and help to establish mutual trust. They can provide parents with more complete information about literacy development and their own child's progress. Initial discussions with the parents of nursery children may take place during home visits before the child starts at school when parents can tell staff about the child's present experiences with print. If parents are asked to compile a pre-entry book with their child this can make a significant contribution to their child's understanding of reading. Later records can be used to structure a discussion about the child's development as a reader and parental support for the child's work on reading targets can be enlisted.

Assessment can be a collaborative exercise. All the staff who work with young children can make an active and important contribution to the assessment process. It is unrealistic to expect teachers to notice all the learning events that take place in the classroom. Support staff may notice significant behaviours as they work with children. They can also be included in the planned assessment opportunities. For example they can be responsible for reading conferences and interviews if they know what these entail. Accepting and seeking information about children from other interested adults promote consistency of approach and acknowledge the contribution all adults make to children's learning.

## *Keeping records*

Although there is no statutory requirement to retain the observations, notes of reading interviews, conferences and miscue analyses or copies of reading diaries, book reviews or other examples of children's achievements in reading, SCAA (1995b) suggest that records are helpful for teachers when they are making their summative assessments at the end of a key stage. If assessment materials are retained they can be referred to when discussing progress with parents and, if passed on to the child's next teacher, can contribute towards continuity of learning for the child. They are a rich source of information and will indicate the breadth of children's reading experience as well as development in the key skills.

Many schools keep a record of work for each child. As they are added to each year they help staff to build up a complete picture of each child's progress over time and are a useful reference for staff. Children's reading records can include:

- teacher observations;
- the results of planned assessment opportunities;
- checklists;
- pupil self-assessments;
- information gained from parents or carers;
- information from other adults who work with the child;
- a record of targets set during reading interviews;
- pieces of writing that reveal something about the child as a reader;
- a record of all the books read over a school year;
- reading summaries; and
- test results.

## *School portfolios*

School portfolios contain annotated examples taken from pupil records from different year groups. They are accompanied by a brief commentary about the context, what the extract shows and why it was selected. The examples can be photocopies rather than actual records if this is easier. School collections provide information about the agreed ways of working and assessment methods and can serve as exemplars for new members of staff and supply teachers. They also record examples of good practice in teaching and assessment that can be referred to by all staff. Examples of miscue analysis, pages from a child's reading journal, records of reading targets and action taken could all be included in a school portfolio.

## Summative assessment

Summative assessment is a summary of what each child can do, knows and understands. It is usually made at a transition point such as on entry to school, when children change classes and at the end of a key stage. The results of summative assessments are passed on to parents, the child's next teacher, the headteacher, governors, the LEA and statutory bodies.

## *Baseline assessment*

From September 1998 it will be a statutory requirement for primary schools to use an accredited baseline assessment scheme with all 4 and 5-year-old children when they first start school. Baseline assessment has two purposes. To

- provide information to help teachers to plan effectively to meet children's individual learning needs; and
- measure children's attainment, using one or more numerical outcomes which can be used in later value-added analyses of children's progress (SCAA, 1997b, p. 3).

Baseline assessments are intended to inform reception teachers about pupils' preschool experience and their early achievements so that they can accommodate individual needs into their planning. They may also lead to the early identification of special educational needs and more able children. By referring to the results of these early assessments, when later assessments are made, schools and teachers will be able to measure the progress children make in school.

Schools will be able to select the baseline assessment they use from a list of accredited schemes. They may be able to choose one produced by their local education authority. All schemes will include assessments of language and literacy, mathematics and personal and social development. In the guidance produced by SCAA (1997a) it is suggested that the following aspects of reading should be assessed:

### *Reading for meaning and enjoyment*

- Know how to hold books, turn pages and use illustrations and memory to retell a story;
- predict words and phrases that make sense in context;
- use memory to recognise and read two words in a familiar text; and
- read a large portion of text accurately.

### *Letter knowledge*

- Recognise his or her own name;

- recognise five letters by shape and sound;
- recognise fifteen letters by shape and sound; and
- recognise all letters by shape and sound.

### Phonological awareness

- Recite familiar rhymes;
- recognise initial sounds;
- associate sounds with patterns in rhyme; and
- demonstrate knowledge of sound sequences in words.

SCAA expect that most children in their first weeks in reception classes will be able to achieve the first three items in each scale and less than 20% of children will be able to fulfil the requirements for the fourth item. The fourth item in each scale corresponds to level 1 of the National Curriculum.

## National Curriculum tests

All children in their final year of Key Stage 1 are legally required to be tested. Most of these children will be 7 years old and in year 2. The National Curriculum assessment arrangements include a combination of tests and teacher assessment. The exact format and resources used in the tests may change from year to year but the general arrangements are similar. To assess reading formally children select a book to read from three or four taken from the booklist provided. They have a preliminary discussion with the teacher about the book. They then read aloud to the teacher and, after the reading, talk about what they have read. Children have to demonstrate their ability to read with accuracy, fluency and a sense of meaning and engage in a discussion which provides evidence of their understanding and ability to respond to what they read. Specific criteria are provided to help teachers determine which level children reach. Children who are expected to attain level 2 are given a reading comprehension test. Those who achieve the highest grade on the level-2 task and test take the level-3 comprehension test. Although the tests are time consuming they are not professionally demanding. They are intended to resemble some of the reading activities that normally take place in the class. The processes the children go through and the organisation of the children can be similar to some of the routines that are regularly employed in the class such as taking a reading sample.

## Standardised reading tests

In addition to the National Curriculum tests and tasks, schools and LEAs may administer reading tests. These may be given to individual children, particularly those who are experiencing difficulty in becoming readers, or to all the children at the end of each school year. The tests selected should suit the purpose for which they are being used so the results will be useful to the teacher and the child. Tests given to children who are giving cause for concern should provide information about

* why the child is failing;
* the nature of the child's difficulties; and
* the possible focus for the intervention

so the child can be given specialised help.

Reading tests used to monitor school standards and that are given to all children should be

* suited to the age group and the school;
* straightforward and quick to administer; and
* informative in the way the school or LEA wants.

The most popular tests administered to large groups of children generally provide teachers with a reading age, reading quotient or standardised score. Simply, these numbers show whether children are reading at an average, below-average or above-average level for their age. This information usually confirms what teachers already know rather than providing any new insights that can be used to inform teaching. They do not provide diagnostic information about strengths and weaknesses or progress that can be used to plan for individual children's requirements. Many tests are culturally and linguistically inappropriate to children today since most were compiled some time ago. They may require children to recognise old-fashioned words in artificial contexts. Because of their limitations, most schools regard reading tests as complementary to other methods of assessment which do provide detailed information teachers can use.

## Formal teacher assessment

This refers to the statutory requirement for teachers to make an assessment of children's learning towards the end of each key stage. Teacher assessment is an essential part of the National Curriculum assessment requirements and the results of teacher assessments are reported alongside the test results. Both have equal status and provide complementary information about children's attainment. Teacher assessment should be based on the formative assessments undertaken throughout each key stage of learning. The summary can then take account of progress as well as achievement in a range of contexts and will therefore provide a broad picture of the child's strengths and weaknesses. This complements the limited information about attainment levels provided by tests. When making teacher assessments the teacher will make a 'best fit' judgement of the level of attainment reached based on the level descriptions by drawing on pupil records. These judgements can be moderated by referring to the school portfolio, the Exemplification of Standards (SCAA, 1995b) and discussion and comparison of standards with other staff.

## *Reports*

In many schools teachers prepare a formal summary of progress at the end of each school year. The information about children's reading development teachers collect using all or some of the methods described in this chapter should enable teachers to make comprehensive, useful and informative summaries at the end of a term, a year or a key stage. This is then passed on to the child's next teacher and shared with parents in the child's written report. It may also be shared with pupils. Reports draw on all the assessment data that have been collected during the year. They should indicate the breadth of children's reading experience, the key skills they are developing and their awareness and use of features of print as identified in the programmes of study.

## Conclusion

Assessment has a number of purposes and audiences. The most important purpose is to benefit children and help them to develop their abilities. Consequently the most important audiences are those who have direct contact with the children and are responsible for their learning. Gathering sufficient information to understand what children know and can do involves using a range of assessment techniques over a period of time. It is then important to use this information productively so that assessment becomes an integral part of the cycle of teaching and learning and enables teachers to plan ahead for children's learning requirements.

## Further reading

Bearne, E. (1998) *Making Progress in English*, Routledge, London.

Nutbrown, C. (1997) *Recognising Early Literacy Development: Assessing Children's Achievements*, Paul Chapman Publishing, London.

Sainsbury, M. (1996) *Tracking Significant Achievement in Primary English*, Hodder & Stoughton, London.

SCAA (1995) *Consistency in Teacher Assessment: Exemplification of Standards*, SCAA, London.

SCAA (1996) *Standardised Literacy Tests in Primary Schools: Their Use and Usefulness*, SCAA, London.

# 8

# Planning for reading

## Introduction

Planning draws on all a teacher knows and understands about reading, about classroom management, about ways of working with children, about the children in her class and about the statutory requirements. When planning the teacher considers what has to be learned and how it will be taught. Clear, detailed plans ensure all aspects of each subject are covered and that there is progression, balance, breadth, coherence and continuity in the curriculum that is offered to pupils. Medium and short-term plans have clear aims and contain activities that are sequenced and structured. The way in which the activities are organised provides children with opportunities to acquire, practise and consolidate their reading in ways that are appropriate to them.

Planning is not a simple undertaking. However it is worth the effort. A coherent, systematic plan for reading development which guides one's teaching is a valuable resource. Even more importantly it should result in greater or easier success at learning to read for children. This chapter explains the processes involved at each stage of planning and considers what might be included in long, medium and short-term plans for reading.

## The necessity of planning for reading

Until recently preparing thorough plans for reading development was uncommon. Although teachers planned carefully for learning in other areas of the curriculum, plans for reading often consisted of little more than identifying which children would read each day. It has become clear that planning for reading is necessary and beneficial. It can help teachers to

- cover the requirements of the National Curriculum, the *Desirable Outcomes for Learning* and the *Framework for Teaching;*

- translate the statutory requirements into teachable units;
- provide a coherent and structured guide for teaching;
- build up a resource bank of purposeful activities;
- develop clarity about what should be taught, when it should be taught, how it should be taught and why;
- help those who feel insecure about teaching reading to feel more confident;
- ensure continuity and progression;
- recognise where English enriches, supports and is integrated with other curriculum areas; and
- identify possible assessment opportunities.

All these are important if children are to make good progress towards fluency in reading.

## The context for planning

### *Using the statutory guidance*

Throughout this book close attention has been paid to the statutory requirements for reading in the early years, the *Desirable Outcomes for Children's Learning* (SCAA, 1996a) and *English in the National Curriculum* (DfE, 1995). The curriculum map for reading outlined in the *Framework for Teaching* (DfEE, 1998) has also been referred to. All these documents have a significant influence on planning for reading in the early years.

The National Curriculum and the *Desirable Outcomes for Children's Learning* outline a series of logically sequenced goals for children's learning but do not determine how these aims should be achieved. The *Framework for Teaching* contains detailed guidance about the content of the curriculum for reading and writing throughout the primary years. Together, these three documents give a clear indication of the progression, balance, breadth, coherence and continuity in the curriculum that are needed term by term and year by year from the nursery to the end of Key Stage 2.

The statutory demands are guides for planning rather than complete curriculum documents. The statements about reading in the programme of study do not represent the complexity of all that is required in order to become an effective reader. For example acquiring 'a vocabulary of words recognised and understood automatically and quickly' (DfE, 1995 p. 7) begins and develops through experiences with books, listening and watching as stories and books are shared, becoming aware of and using words in the environment, seeing relevant words frequently, experimenting with words in personal writing, discussing words and letters with experienced readers, playing games with words and letters as well as many other activities. Similarly the *Framework for Teaching* states what children should be learning but does not prescribe how. Both documents provide the content of the curriculum but do not stipulate how the content is to be distributed over each term or the tasks and activities the pupils will undertake.

Official documents may be the starting point for planning and will influence what is taught and learned. However it is clear that schools and teachers are free to make a number of choices relating to teaching style, content and resources before children receive the curriculum for reading. The teacher's own plans translate the statutory requirements into workable activities and routines in the classroom.

## School documentation

All the planning teachers do should be informed by the overall aims for education that have been identified by the school in their teaching and learning documents and the overall aims for reading as set out in the school's reading policy. Although reading policies are a statement of intent rather than a teaching plan they should influence teachers' work in the classroom. They usually begin with a summary of the schools' aims for reading development which have been agreed by all the staff. They may contain sections which outline the resources which are used, common classroom practices, some elements of organisation such as the use of volunteers, monitoring procedures and arrangements for particular groups of children. A good reading policy is intended to result in a consistent approach to reading across the school. This will happen if it is consulted by teachers as they plan. For example, if the agreed aims for reading included

- the development of independence and autonomy;
- the use of the knowledge, skills and abilities at a functional level; and
- the use of knowledge, skills and abilities for personal satisfaction

then each teacher would want to make sure that what is planned and how it is to be organised fitted in with these intentions.

## Crosscurricular links

Children read across the whole curriculum to gain information and ideas from a range of sources. They may read workbooks, worksheets, reference books, maps, pictures and text on the computer. Using their reading skills as they play and work helps children to see the usefulness of reading. Children are also expected to write in many situations in school and writing helps to consolidate children's understanding of print. The opportunities that exist for developing and using reading across the curriculum should be identified and considered as part of the whole reading curriculum children receive.

## Classroom management

What is planned and the curriculum the children receive is influenced by the way the teacher manages her classroom. The teacher's knowledge, her way of working and the environment in which she works will affect the activities she plans and the way these are arranged. All the following have a direct influence on planning:

- understanding of techniques for teaching reading;
- teaching style;
- the routines and structures in place;
- the use of time;
- the way in which the physical environment is arranged;
- the resources available;
- children's behaviour; and
- the adults who work with the children.

Activities and experiences in themselves do not always lead to learning. It is easy to occupy children with low-level, repetitive tasks which ask them to practise and repeat what they already know but which do not extend learning. Activities need to be planned with specific learning intentions in mind. Effective activities are those which develop existing abilities and lead to new learning.

Considering how to make best use of the children's and the teacher's time is an important part of planning since the efficient use of time enables the teacher to spend more time working with pupils. As she plans the teacher will consider when to use whole-class and group teaching and for what purpose. The activities the children carry out independently will be selected with care. By thinking ahead about the demands they will make and how the children will be grouped for different activities, the teacher will be in a better position to make good use of the children's time and feel confident she will be able to give focused attention to groups and individuals.

The success of what is planned may depend on the way the classroom is organised and managed. When children have easy access to resources, are familiar with working independently and collaboratively and know what to do when they finish an activity there is a greater likelihood that the learning that is planned will be realised. Careful forethought about the implications of the plans for organisation and resources is likely to lead to an atmosphere of order and purposeful work in the classroom.

## Planning for reading

### *Long-term planning*

Long-term plans contain a broad overview of the curriculum that is to be presented to children during their time in the nursery and throughout the school. They reflect the school's policies and priorities as well as the statutory requirements and identify the long-term goals for the children's learning. They show what all the staff of the school are working towards. Long-term plans may also indicate links between different subject areas and learning experiences. Producing long-term plans helps to ensure children receive a broad and balanced curriculum and that there is progression and continuity over an extended period. They will identify the range and variety of experiences children will be given over a number of years. Some of the learning opportunities, such as story times, will be offered continuously; others will be planned to fit in with particular themes or events that occur during each year. All the experiences should be designed to enable children to achieve the desirable outcomes and the National Curriculum level descriptions. They will also fit in with the *Framework for Teaching* by indicating, for example, when children will be introduced to dictionaries, undertake an in-depth author study and begin to work on alphabetical order.

The long-term aims for developing each of the following aspects of reading can be identified in the long-term plan:

- the key skills
- range
- response
- standard English and language study.

Long-term plans should be an established structure and should be frequently referred to by staff and updated regularly.

### *Medium-term planning*

The starting point for medium-term planning is the clear identification of the goals for pupil learning for each half-term. Each of these intentions is then used to guide the selection of teaching methods and learning opportunities that will make up the reading curriculum. For example, if reception children are expected to learn 'that words can be written down to be read again for a wide range of purposes' (DfEE, 1998, p. 18) they will need to see words being written and return to and read these words at another time. The experiences that will help them to do this might include shared writing, scribing, shared reading, writing names, playing games using sets of name cards and exploring the use of writing in role play. These activities will be included in the medium-term plan.

Much of the work planned for reading in the early years will begin with a book for children that is available as an enlarged text. It should be selected for its relevance and interest to the children, the potential it offers for learning to read and the way it supports the teacher's learning intentions for the medium term. A single book or several books on similar themes or by the same author may be explored over half a term.

After the learning intentions have been examined, the texts selected and a number of suitable activities identified, the next stage is to arrange the activities in a coherent order. Different activities will require different forms of organisation. A balance of whole-class, group and individual teaching and opportunities for crosscurricular reinforcement and independent and collaborative work will make it easier to manage the children's learning. Times for the children to reflect on their learning and for the teacher to assess their progress can be included in the plan.

Children's learning rarely happens in a straightforward linear fashion, nor do children necessarily learn what their teachers intend. They may learn other related things. They may build on prior experiences and knowledge in unpredictable ways. They sometimes seem to know things adults might think were too complicated and conversely can appear to have difficulty with what appears to be simple. Although children may not learn A then B then C, teachers need to have a sense of A comes before B in order to ensure progression in the long term. So in order for the scheme of work to be helpful, manageable and workable it is necessary to organise it so it can be read as a developmental sequence of activities.

## Short-term planning

Short-term planning translates a scheme of work for half a term into the working reality of each classroom. It is constructed on a weekly basis and may be amended each day. It contains a weekly overview of activities and daily plans. Successive week's plans are influenced by the results of the teacher's assessments of pupils and evaluations of teaching. Short-term planning should take account of the particular needs of individual classes and children. Its purpose is to ensure that day-to-day teaching is based on clear and realisable aims and is effective.

For students, daily plans may be fairly detailed. They will usually begin with a clear statement of what is to be learned by the pupils during the session and include references to content, organisation and structure. They may also specify what the teacher will do, what the children will be expected to do, how the children will be grouped and organised, approximate timings for various parts of the session and the resources that will be needed.

Short-term planning is able to take account of the different needs and abilities of the pupils in the class. The teacher may expect all the children to undertake the same activities but expect different outcomes from some individuals. Alternatively similar tasks may be presented in different ways depending on the level of support the children require. When working with groups, the teacher's inputs can be differentiated to suit different levels of experience and followed up with tasks that are suited to the needs of the group. Particular attention may need to be given to the children with special educational needs, more able children and children for whom English is an additional language and, where necessary, the curriculum should be adapted to ensure their learning. Age, interests, learning style, gender and prior experiences may also necessitate differentiation. Each of the following variables can be altered in order to provide differentiated work:

- the activity – different activities can lead to the same outcome;
- the outcome – different children can produce different responses to the same task;
- the input – provided by the teacher before the children begin the activity;
- the support – provided by adults and peers during the activity;
- the resources – more, less or different resources can be used;
- the criteria for success – can be different for different groups of children; and
- the intention – whether learning is to be explored, practised, consolidated or extended.

Differentiation should result in an appropriate match between learner needs and activities. Well matched tasks allow children to exhibit what they already know while taking them on to new ground. They should result in pupil achievement and satisfaction so that children develop positive attitudes towards learning and confidence in themselves as learners.

When constructing the weekly plan the teacher will be thinking about the type of activities she is offering to the children. She will want to vary the opportunities they have for acquisition, practice, consolidation and extension. If there are too many practice or consolidation tasks the children will find the curriculum undemanding and routine. If the children are expected to move too quickly from introductory activities to extension work their learning will be fragmented and incomplete. Making careful choices based on the experience of the children and their learning requirements will help to ensure all the children make progress at a pace that is suited to their needs.

For each daily planned activity, the teacher needs to be clear about why she is asking children to undertake it, what the children will understand as the purpose of the activity, the potential difficulties of each task and the teaching that may be required. To be effective, each activity should be

- *focused* – have clear learning intentions and build on prior learning;
- *organised* – to enable the aims to be achieved and to make good use of teacher and pupil time;
- *matched* – to the learning capabilities of each child; and
- *purposeful* – so that children will understand the substance and purpose of what they do.

Short-term planning provides the opportunity to consider these issues and to offer children enriching and successful learning experiences that not only teach children how to read but also

- ensure children's encounters with print are purposeful and meaningful;
- develop positive attitudes to reading; and
- make reading relevant and important to children.

## *Evaluation*

In order to know if the teaching and the curriculum that are planned and provided are helping children to reach the learning intentions that were established at the beginning of the planning cycle, children's learning in response to the activities has to be monitored. Regular and systematic evaluation through observation, discussion with pupils, analysis of their work and pupil appraisals of their own learning enables the teacher to consider the appropriateness of the curriculum she is providing, to see whether her aims are being realised and to make judgements about the nature and quality of pupil learning. Daily and weekly monitoring helps the teacher to be responsive to all the children's individual learning needs. The teacher will be expecting the children to achieve her aims, looking for demonstrations of progress in reading and expecting children to show signs of positive attitudes and growing confidence. If these signs of progress are not evident, it may be that after reflection, the teacher needs to adapt the aims, activities or organisation contained in her planning until she creates an environment in which every child can develop.

## Planning examples

There are many ways to record planning. Schools often devise a system which suits them and everyone develops a particular preference for a format they find most useful. The remainder of this chapter gives some practical examples of planning for reading in the early years. They are only examples and would need to be adapted to meet particular circumstances. They show how the requirements of the *Framework for Teaching*, the National Curriculum and the *Desirable Outcomes for Children's Learning* can be addressed from nursery through to year 3.

### *Nursery and reception plans*

With very young children teachers may wish to base some of their work around established learning areas and common resources before planning particular activities to teach children about reading. In the first instance they may list what the resources in the class offer in regard to reading. Some of these ideas could be in continuous use; others could be used during particular themes. This list could then be used a resource to draw from when planning for children in nursery and reception classes, as the following example indicates:

*Sand*
Make patterns, letters and words; record their experiences in pictures and writing; read about their experiences from displays and in made and published books; say, sing and learn rhymes about sand

*Water*
Record their experiences in pictures and writing; use plastic, foam and wooden letters; read about their experiences from displays and in made and published books; say, sing and learn rhymes about water

*Blocks*
Record their experiences in pictures and writing, use books as a source of information for making their structures

*Construction*
Make and follow plans; use books as a source of information for making their models; make models connected with stories

*Writing area*
Practise the language of books; through writing become familiar with print, letters and communication through writing; use diaries, notebooks and blank books; refer to alphabet books and dictionaries become confident with writing, words and letters

*Role play*
Recreate familiar stories; explore character and plot and read signs and posters; use a range of written materials; practise reading and writing in context

*Music*
Recognise patterns and rhymes; use print and symbols to record and sing songs; introduce syllabification through clapping rhythms

*Creative activities*
Use a book as a stimulus for activities; paint scenes and characters from books; make labels and captions for models books; become aware of detail and pattern; experiment with mark making; print patterns, letters and words

*Games*
Follow instructions; play games that are linked with familiar books; sort and match letters and words

*Reading area*
Enjoy books independently and with others; listen to stories, rhymes and poems; retell familiar stories; use and learn book language; become familiar with different formats; understand that pictures and words convey meaning; recognise familiar words; sequence known stories using cards; select and enjoy books independently

*Outdoor play*
Recreate familiar stories; make patterns and letters using outdoor resources; play games involving songs and rhymes

*Maths area*
Identify symbols; read books about mathematical activities

*Malleable materials*
Make letter shapes and words; use and write recipes

*Small world play*
Represent known stories; create stories using puppets and toys; make labels and captions for models; use books to inform play

*Technology*
Refer to books for ideas; record planning and outcomes

*ICT*
Explore letters on the keyboard; use programs about letters and words; follow print from left to right

Medium-term planning can be recorded as a sequence of objectives, as in the example that follows. Here the aims for each term have been derived from the *Desirable Outcomes for Children's Learning* (SCAA, 1996a). The aims show progression over the three terms children spend in the nursery:

| *Term 1* | *Term 2* | *Term 3* |
|---|---|---|
| Children listen to stories | Children join in with stories | Children read stories with others |
| Children use their names in a variety of situations | Children recognise their names | Children recognise individual letters in their names |
| Children enjoy looking at books | Children choose to use books | Children can say why they enjoy favourite books |
| Children become aware of the enjoyment of reading | Children recognise that reading is necessary in everyday life | Children are familiar with many of the uses of reading |

Further detail could be added to this list of termly objectives to provide ideas for medium and short-term plans, as in the following example:

*Learning objective* Children enjoy looking at books
*Area-based learning* Books, tapes and props in the book area; story times; display popular books
*Planned activities* Revisit known stories; use stories in role-play area; use books as starting points for children's own stories
*Adult support* Talk about books and stories; model dialogue based on known stories; model personal stories

Figure 8.1 shows a medium-term plan for language and literacy for three weeks in a nursery where the children were exploring the theme

| Focus Pattern | Time span 3 weeks | Class Nursery |
|---|---|---|
| Area of learning Language and literacy | | |

| *Learning intentions* | *Resources* | *Activities* |
|---|---|---|
| To develop an awareness of sound patterns | Large charts of rhymes and poems | Saying and singing rhymes and poems |
| | Dr Seuss Books | Encourage children to identify rhymes |
| | Stories with repetitive refrains | Make up new nursery rhymes |
| | | Encourage children to join in with refrains |
| | | Tapes in the listening area |
| | A set of children's name cards | Think of words to rhyme with children's names |
| | | Clap the rhythms of children's names |
| | Musical instruments | Create patterns of sounds with instruments |
| | | Record musical patterns |

*Evaluation*

The children enjoyed the rhyming activities.

They were able to join in with refrains such as 'Trip, trap, trip, trap'.

They will need further experiences to isolate onsets such as *tr* from *-ip* and *-ap* and to appreciate that changing the vowel changes the word.

Work on rhythm and rhymes will continue throughout the planned themes.

**Figure 8.1**   Medium-term plan for language and literacy in a nursery class

| Date 2–6 May | Theme Food | Class Nursery | | | |
|---|---|---|---|---|---|
| | Monday | Tuesday | Wednesday | Thursday | Friday |
| Imaginative play area | Fruit and vegetable stall – all week | | | | |
| Science | Making cakes | Comparing fruits | Making sandwiches | Comparing vegetables | Classifying foods |
| Construction | Making an allotment | Making a lighthouse | Making an allotment | Making a farm | Making a farm |
| Maths | Weighing and balance | Sorting | Shapes | Sorting | Sorting |
| Language and literacy | *The Shopping Basket* | *The Lighthouse Keeper's Lunch* | Listing foods for picnics | *The Enormous Turnip* | *The Lighthouse Keeper's Lunch* |
| Music | *The Queen of Hearts* | 1, 2, 3, 4, 5 | 'I'm A Little Teapot' | 'One Potato, Two Potato' | 'The Farmer's in his Den' |
| Writing area | Lists | Fruit books | Sandwich sequences | Lists | Food books |
| Creative work | Play-doh cakes | Collage with seeds | Drawing fruit | Collage | Printing with vegetables |
| Outdoor play | 'The Farmer's in his Den' | Climbing frame – lighthouse | 'Oranges and Lemons' | Climbing frame – lighthouse | Picnic equipment |
| Water | Different-sized containers | Boats | Enact *The Lighthouse Keeper's Lunch* | Boats | Different-sized containers |
| Sand | Wet sand and cake moulds | Different-sized containers | Farm equipment | Wet sand and cake moulds | Farm equipment |

**Figure 8.2**  Weekly plan for a nursery class

of pattern. Figure 8.2 is an example of a weekly plan on the theme of food for a nursery. It covers all areas of the curriculum but demonstrates how reading and interest in books can be fostered in a range of activities. For example on Monday the children would have experience of sharing a story, exploring the story further through role play, writing shopping lists, reading recipes and becoming aware of patterns of sounds in rhymes and songs.

The final example of planning for the under-5s is a daily plan for the same nursery. This shows how the adults supported the language and literacy activities and how time was allocated for the children to talk about their learning:

**Daily plan**

*Time    Activities, organisation, adult involvement*

9.00     Registration, planning, change home reading books
         Children to select from the prepared activities
         5 children to bake with Celia
         Demonstrate shopping lists in the writing area

9.30     Outside, play 'The Farmer's in his Den'

10.00    Monitor and support children with Play-doh, writing area
         and weighing

10.30    Outside final game of 'The Farmer's in his Den' and start
         to tidy up

10.45    Snack time
         Share cakes
         Children who have made cakes to tell the rest of the class
         how they did this
         Discuss work undertaken during the morning – children
         to show shopping lists

11.00    Tidy up

11.10    Story – *The Shopping Basket*
         Rhyme – *The Queen of Hearts*

11.30    Home time

Figure 8.3 shows a sample taken from the medium-term planning for literacy hour work in a reception class. The plans are based on the text *Not Now Bernard* (McKee, 1980) for which an enlarged text version is also available. The work is divided into word, sentence and text-level intentions. It shows how development in reading, writing, speaking and listening will be covered over a period of five weeks.

| Book title | Main elements to explore in the text | Time span | Year group |
|---|---|---|---|
| *Not Now Bernard* | • Imaginary monsters<br>• Communication, being heard<br>• Structure and pattern in the story<br>• Other books by David McKee<br>• Writing fiction | 5 weeks | Reception |

| Learning intentions | Texts and resources | Activities and outcomes |
|---|---|---|
| *Word Level*<br>• To be able to read the title and identify these words in the text<br>• To begin to identify words that begin with *b* and *n*<br>• To list words beginning with *b* and *n*<br>• To be able to identify 'said' and spell it accurately | Multiple copies of *Not Now Bernard*<br><br>Big book *Not Now Bernard*<br><br>Sequencing cards | *Reading activities*<br>• Whole-class shared reading of enlarged text<br>• Group reading<br>• Make story props<br>• Use story props to retell story<br>• Record retellings on to tape<br>• Children record their readings of the story |
| *Sentence level*<br>• To understand that a word consists of a string of letters with a space before the next<br>• To identify full stops in the text<br>• To identify capital letters in the text | Other books by David McKee:<br>*Elmer*<br>*Tusk Tusk*<br>*The Monster and the Teddy Bear* | *Writing activities*<br>• Make a large class book based on the story *Not Now Susan, Not Now Ali*, etc.<br>• Draft, edit and publish writing for the class book<br>• Write descriptions of monsters for display<br>• Write review quotes for the book |
| *Text level*<br>• To become familiar with the text<br>• To retell the story by sequencing events<br>• To become familiar with 'then', 'next', 'after', 'at last' as the vocabulary used in stories<br>• To explore Bernard's experiences | IT concept keyboard overlay<br>Role-play area Bernard's House<br>Monster masks | *Speaking and listening activities*<br>• Oral retelling of the story<br>• Children to comment and respond to the written descriptions<br>• Share responses to the story |

**Figure 8.3** Medium-term planning for a reception class

**Book title**
*A Balloon for Grandad* by Nigel Gray

**Main elements to explore in the text**
- Emotions associated with losing a treasured possession
- Being separated from someone you love
- Vivid imagery and descriptive language

**Time span**
6 weeks

**Year group**
One

| Learning intentions | Texts and resources | Activities and outcomes |
| --- | --- | --- |
| **Book level** | | |
| • To be able to describe why front cover is important<br>• To be able to locate the small extract illustration in the main picture<br>• To be able to name the title, author and illustrator of the book and find this information in the book<br>• To explore the relationship between text and illustrations on a page | Multiple copies of *A Balloon for Grandad*<br><br>Big book *A Balloon for Grandad*<br><br>A selection of the children's favourite books | • Make a group list of favourite books identifying both title and author<br>• Produce illustrations that match sentences when writing<br>• Write book blurbs for own balloon story |
| **Word Level** | | |
| • To be able to use descriptive vocabulary to describe the balloon and its movement<br>• To identify words that describe location<br>• To read colour words accurately<br>• To spell colour words correctly<br>• To be able to locate and read function words *and, it, the, he* in the text | 'Colour Bingo' game | • Look for words and phrases to describe the balloon in the text<br>• Draw balloons and use descriptive vocabulary to describe shape, size, material, movement, etc. Write words onto balloons<br>• Brainstorm a list of words associated with locations and setting |

| Learning intentions | Texts and resources | Activities and outcomes |
| --- | --- | --- |
| | | • Match written words to colours |
| | | • Play 'Colour Bingo' |
| | | • Make a chart recording colour preferences |
| | | • Add new words to class word bank |
| **Sentence level** | | |
| • To be able to structure own story writing in simple sentences | | • Write own balloon journey story |
| • To be able to distinguish between capital and lower-case letters | | • Edit writing for use of capital letters and full stops |
| • To be able to use capital and lower-case letters appropriately | | • Use letter stencils and magnetic letters to sort letters into upper and lower case |
| • To be able to read simple sentences and provide substitutes for missing words | | • Read sentences from the text and think of suitable substitutes for missing words |
| • To know the term full stop | | |
| **Language level** | 'My Cat' – a poem by Nigel Gray | • Use balloon description words to write a group poem about an inflated balloon |
| • To be able to write a letter in the first person | Assorted balloons | • Model letter writing through shared writing |
| • To be able to structure a letter to a family member | Collection of letters | • Brainstorm a list of alternatives to *said* |
| • To be able to compare the layout of a poem and a story | | |
| • To be able to write a collaborative group poem | | |
| • To be able to use alternatives to *said* | | |

| Learning intentions | Texts and resources | Activities and outcomes |
|---|---|---|
| **Literal level** <br><br>• To be able to use text and illustrations to sequence the journey of the balloon <br>• To be able to look closely at the illustrations to add detail to the text <br>• To use illustrations to support reading <br>• To be able to match location descriptions to their correct illustrations <br>• To be able to use information in books and atlases to find out about geographical locations | Sequencing cards <br>Story prompt cards <br>Illustrations and words | • Use story prompt cards to sequence the story <br>• Use sequencing cards to support oral retelling of the story <br>• Produce a group story map charting the journey of the balloon <br>• Sequence sentences in pairs <br>• Matching words to illustrations <br>• Make a list of vocabulary to describe different geographical locations |
| **Inferential level** <br><br>• To be able to predict what might happen to the balloon in the course of its journey <br>• To be able to talk about the likelihood of a balloon travelling such a distance <br>• To recognise how Sam's emotions change throughout the text and identify the evidence we have for this <br>• To be able to predict exactly what Grandad Abdulla would say when the balloon arrived <br>• To predict what might happen in a sequel to *A Balloon for Grandad* | Laminated speech-bubble pictures of Sam and his dad | • Complete conversation speech bubbles in illustrations of Sam and his dad, emphasising the use of language which expresses emotions <br>• Compose a sequel to the book |

| Learning intentions | Texts and resources | Activities and outcomes |
|---|---|---|
| **Evaluative level** <br> • To be able to talk about a favourite illustration and justify the choice <br> • To be able to talk about favourite parts of the book <br> • To be able to say which parts of the book they disliked and why <br> • To discuss what could be changed in the book and why | | • Reproduce a favourite illustration using pastels <br> • Write own version of the story for a class anthology |

**Figure 8.4**  Medium-term planning for a year-1 class

| Class | Title | Time available |
|---|---|---|
| Year 3 | English Reading | 15 hours over 3 weeks |

*Relevant sections of the National Curriculum programmes of study*

1a, c, d   Pupils will be encouraged to develop as enthusiastic, independent and reflective readers, with texts that extend thinking, with more complex narrative structures. The texts will be traditional stories.

2a, b   Pupils should be taught to extend their phonic and graphic knowledge to include more complex patterns and irregularities. Pupils should be taught to consider in detail the quality and depth of what they read.

3   Pupils should be introduced to the organisational, structural and presentational features of different types of texts.

| *Activities (what the pupils will do)* | *Key elements of learning (what the pupils will learn)* |
|---|---|
| **Pupils will** | **Pupils will** |
| Participate in shared reading – week 1 *Why Flies Buzz* retold by Brenda Parkes, weeks 2 and 3 – *Why Frog and Snake Can't Be Friends* | Develop their reading fluency through supported reading |
| | Develop their ability to read with expression and understanding through assuming the roles of the main characters |
| Discuss their understanding and response to the texts | |
| Identify and compare story openings during class discussions | Begin to appreciate how punctuation helps with understanding text |
| Read other traditional stories during guided and personal reading | Appreciate that stories can begin in different ways |
| | Deepen their understanding of story structure |
| Participate in guided group reading | Develop their appreciation of different story genres and associated elements |
| Investigate recurring character types in traditional stories | |
| Make collections of story openings | |
| Make collections of character types | Appreciate stereotypical characteristics of good and bad characters |
| Compile a story board to identify elements of plot in traditional stories | Learn about the power of adjectives to enliven texts |
| | Appreciate that dictionaries and thesauri can provide alternative words |
| Investigate heroes and villains in TV programmes, films and books | Revise the long vowel phoneme *u* |

Develop their reading strategies by combining context cues with initial letters, phonic cues, syllabification and illustrations
Develop their ability to make appropriate predictions about unknown words

*Resources*
Big books
Group readers
Photocopies of pages from the texts
Materials to make language games

Write a description of a hero/heroine and a villain
Make comparisons between character types
Identify adjectives in texts
Complete cloze texts with adjectives
Experiment with adjectives in shared and personal writing
Make collections of adjectives to describe good and bad characters
Use the collections for their writing, to identify spelling patterns and practise syllabification
Identify the long vowel phoneme *u* (*ue*, *oo*, *ew*) and exceptions in shared and individual texts
Find their own words containing the long *u* phoneme
Undertake a newspaper search for the phoneme *u*
Play word snap with long-vowel phoneme *u* words

*Assessment opportunities*
These will occur during guided group reading sessions

*Organisation*
Whole class for shared reading and plenary sessions
Five ability groups for guided group reading and other group activities
Other available adults Ms C every day, Mrs F Tuesday and Thursday

**Figure 8.5**   Medium-term plan for reading with a year-3 class

**Weekly Plan**

| Group | Monday | Tuesday | Wednesday | Thursday | Friday |
|---|---|---|---|---|---|
| 1 | text level | text level | sentence level | guided group reading | word level |
| 2 | text level | text level | word level | sentence level | guided group reading |
| 3 | sentence level | guided group reading | text level | text level | word level |
| 4 | guided group reading | word level | text level | text level | sentence level |
| 5 | word level | sentence level | guided group reading | reading conferences | text level |

**Figure 8.6**   Weekly plan for group activities in the literacy hour

**Type of session** English   **Date** 26.1.98   **Learning objectives**
*Length of session* 1 hour
*Number in group* 28
*Age* Year 3

Learning objectives:
To appreciate stereotypical characteristics of good and bad characters
To learn about the power of adjectives to enliven texts
To appreciate that dictionaries and thesauri can provide alternative words
To revise the long-vowel phoneme u

| Timing | Teacher input and pupil interaction | Resources |
|---|---|---|
| 20 mins | Shared reading and writing | |
| | Using *Why Frog and Snake Can't Be Friends* discuss the different characteristics of the two main characters | *Why Frog and Snake Can't Be Friends* |
| | Referring to *Anancy and Mr Dry-Bone* and *The True Story of the Three Little Pigs* elicit further character traits | *Anancy and Mr Dry-Bone* *The True Story of the Three Little Pigs* |
| | Model a spider graph which lists the characteristics of heroes/villains | |
| | Identify and discuss adjectives on the chart | |
| 30 mins | Group work | |
| Group 1 | Draw up a chart listing the characteristics of a hero/heroine selected from a familiar book. Work in pairs. Use dictionaries and thesauri to find additional words | Dictionaries and thesauri |
| Group 2 | Draw up a chart listing the characteristics of a hero/heroine selected from a familiar book. Work in pairs | Collection of traditional stories |
| Group 3 | Using the list compiled in shared reading to make adjective word cards to be used for word snap. Additional words to be gathered from books in the reading area | Draft books, card, felt tips |
| Group 4 | Guided group reading of *Anancy and Mr Dry-Bone*. Focus on a sustained and enjoyable read for the group | Group readers *Anancy and Mr Dry-Bone* |

| | | *The True Story of the Three Little Pigs* |
|---|---|---|
| Group 5 | Starting with the word *true* compile a list of long-vowel *u* phoneme words. If time begin to sort these according to letter combinations. As a whole group. (Mrs C) | Computer plus database program |
| | Some children from Group 1 may be able to begin to enter their findings on a database | |
| 10 mins | Plenary session | |
| | Share adjectives used to describe characters. Children to ask for additional suggestions from the class | |

*Notes*

Group 1   Didn't make as good use of the dictionaries and thesauri as I had hoped. Tomorrow demonstrate the use of these resources to the class.

Group 2   Worked well. Tomorrow they could add to their charts using dictionaries and other resources.

Group 3   Worked well. Good standard of presentation. Good response to identifying long *u* phoneme words.

Group 4   The children took *Anancy and Mr Dry Bone* home to finish.

Group 5   Most children remembered their previous work on *u* and were able to contribute to the list. The sorting activity should be completed tomorrow.

**Figure 8.7**   Daily plan for the literacy hour with a year-3 class

## Key Stage 1

The plan for a half-term's work on *A Balloon for Grandad* (Gray, 1994) (Figure 8.4) includes work on developing bibliographic knowledge in addition to word, sentence and text-level activities. The work designed to support children's learning about text-level strategies for reading and to deepen their understanding and appreciation of books has been subdivided into literal, inferential and evaluative outcomes. The plan also includes a section concerned with standard English and language study.

## Key Stage 2

The final examples (Figures 8.5–8.7) are taken from work planned for a year-3 class for a period of three weeks. The examples included here begin with a medium-term plan for the whole period, then a weekly planning summary of group activities and lastly an example of a daily plan for a literacy hour. There are many ways to record planning for reading and each school or teacher will devise a method to suit themselves. Effective plans should indicate what children are expected to learn, how they will learn what is intended and give some indication of the organisational strategies that will be employed. The illustrations in this chapter may have provided readers with some guidance on how this can be done.

## Conclusion

Planning for reading is supported by national and school guidelines which provide teachers with a useful framework. However, effective individual planning begins with reflecting on the expectations, aims and activities that are appropriate for 3–8-year-old pupils. It relies on the teacher's understanding of how children learn and what they need to learn. It is influenced by planning in other curriculum areas and by linking reading with other areas of the curriculum. It depends on the teacher's knowledge of subjects, organisation and management. Planning a successful programme of work makes demands on the full range of professional knowledge and skills teachers have. Once teachers have planned carefully they are in a strong position to implement an effective and motivating sequence of work with their classes and help children to achieve success at learning to become readers.

## Further reading

Ellis, S. and Barrs, M. (1996) *The Core Book*, CLPE, London.

Field, C. and Lally, M. (1996) *Planning for Progress*, Learning by Design, London.

# References

Adams, M. (1990) *Beginning to Read: Thinking and Learning about Print*, MIT Press, Cambridge, MA.

Ahlberg, J. and Ahlberg, A. (1984) *Each Peach Pear Plum*, Viking, London.

Alborough, J. (1992) *Where's My Teddy?*, Walker, London.

Alborough, J. (1994) *It's the Bear!*, Walker, London.

Alexander, R. (1991) *Primary Education in Leeds. Twelfth and Final Report from the Primary Needs Independent Evaluation Project*, University of Leeds, Leeds.

Alexander, R., Rose, J. and Woodhead, C. (1992) *Curriculum Organisation and Classroom Practice in Primary Schools*, Department of Education and Science, Stanmore.

Alexander, R., Willcoks, J. and Kinder, K. (1995) *Versions of Primary Education*, Routledge, London.

Asher, S. (1980) Topic interest and children's reading comprehension, in R. Spiro, B. Bruce and W. Brewer (eds) *Theoretical Issues in Reading Comprehension*, Lawrence Erlbaum Associates, Hillsdale, NJ.

Baker, J. (1991) *Window*, Julia MacRae, London.

Barber, M. (1997) *A Reading Revolution: How We Can Teach Every Child to Read Well. The Preliminary Report of the Literacy Task Force*, The Literacy Task Force, Institute of Education, London.

Barrs, M., Ellis, S., Heaster, H. and Thomas, A. (1988) *The Primary Language Record: Handbook for Teachers*, CLPE, London.

Bearne, E. (1998) *Making Progress in English*, Routledge, London.

Bennett, J. (1991) *Learning to Read with Picture Books* (4th edn), Thimble Press, Stroud.

Bennett, N., Desforges, C., Cockburn, A. and Wilkinson, A. (1984) *The Quality of Pupil Learning Experiences*, Lawrence Erlbaum Associates, Hilllsdale, NJ.

Benton, M. and Fox, G. (1985) *Teaching Literature 9–14*, Oxford University Press, Oxford.

Bissex, G. (1980) *GNYS AT WRK: A Child Learns to Write and Read*, Harvard University Press, Cambridge, MA.

Blake, Q. (1968) *Patrick*, Picture Lions, London.

Briggs, R. (1978) *The Snowman*, Hamish Hamilton, London.

Brooks, G. (1997) Reading standards static for 50 years, *The Times Educational Supplement*, 11 July.

Brown, R. (1981) *A Dark, Dark Tale*, Scholastic, London.

Browne, A. (1986) *Piggybook*, Julia MacRae, London.

Browne, A. (1994) *Zoo*, Red Fox, London.

Browne, A. (1995) *Willy the Wizard*, Red Fox, London.

Browne, A. (1996) *Developing Language and Literacy 3–8*, Paul Chapman Publishing, London.

Burningham, J. (1978) *Mr Gumpy's Outing*, Puffin Books, Harmondsworth.

Burningham, J. (1980) *The Shopping Basket*, Collins, London.

Cairney, T.H. (1994) *Pathways to Literacy*, Cassell, London.

Campbell, J. and Neill, S. (1994) *Curriculum Reform at Key Stage 1*, Longman, London.

Campbell. R. (1982) *Dear Zoo*, Picture Puffin, Harmondsworth.

Campbell, R. (1990) *Reading Together*, Open University Press, Milton Keynes.

Campbell, R. (1995) *Reading in the Early Years Handbook*, Open University Press, Buckingham.

Campbell, R. (1996) *Literacy in Nursery Education*, Trentham Books, Stoke-on-Trent.

Carle, E. (1969) *The Very Hungry Caterpillar*, Hamish Hamilton, London.

Clay, M.M. (1969) Reading errors and self corrective behaviour, *British Journal of Educational Psychology*, Vol. 39, no. 1, pp. 49–56.

Clay, M.M. (1991) *Becoming Literate: The Construction of Inner Control*, Heinemann, Auckland.

Clymer, T.L. (1963) The utility of phonic generalisations in the primary grades, *The Reading Teacher*, no. 16, pp. 252–8.

Cole, B. (1986) *Princess Smartypants*, Picture Lion, London.

Collington, P. (1995) *The Tooth Fairy*, Cape, London.

Dale, P. (1987) *Bet You Can't!*, Walker, London.

DES (1967) *Children and their Primary Schools (The Plowden Report)*, HMSO, London.

DES (1975) *A Language for Life (The Bullock Report)*, HMSO, London.

DES (1988) *National Curriculum Proposals for English for Ages 5 to 11 (The Cox Committee Report Part 1)*, HMSO, London.

DES (1989) *English for Ages 5–16 (The Cox Report)*, HMSO, London.

DfE (1995) *English in the National Curriculum*, HMSO, London.

DfEE (1997) *The Implementation of the National Literacy Strategy*, DfEE, London.

DfEE (1998) *The National Literacy Strategy Framework for Teaching*, DfEE, London.

Dombey, H. (1994) *Words and Worlds: Reading in the Early Years of School*, NATE, Sheffield.

Dr Seuss (1961) *The Cat in the Hat*, Collins, London.

Edwards, V. (1995) *Reading in Multilingual Classrooms*, Reading and Language Information Centre, University of Reading.

Edwards, V., Goodwin, P., Hunt, G., Redfern, A., Rowe, A. and Routh, C. (1996) *Practical Ways to Organise Reading*, Reading and Language Information Centre, University of Reading.

Ellis, S. and Barrs, M. (1996) *The Core Book*, CLPE, London.

Ferreiro, E. and Teberosky, A. (1983) *Literacy before Schooling*, Heinemann, London.

Field, C. and Lally, M. (1996) *Planning for Progress*, Learning by Design, London.

Freire, P. (1972) *Cultural Action for Freedom*, Penguin, Harmondsworth.

French, F. (1991) *Anancy and Mr Dry-Bone*, Frances Lincoln, London.

Frith, U. (1980) Unexpected spelling problems. In U. Frith (ed) *Cognitive Processes in Spelling*, Academic Press, London.

Galton, M. (1995) Do you really want to cope with thirty lively children and become an effective primary teacher? In J. Moyles (ed) *Beginning Teaching: Beginning Learning*, Open University Press, Buckingham.

Galton, M., Simon, B. and Croll, P. (1980) *Progress and Performance in the Primary Classroom*, Routledge, London.

Goodman, K. (1975) The reading process. In F. Gollasch (ed) (1982) *Language and Literacy: The Selected Writings of Kenneth S. Goodman, Vol. 1*, Routledge & Kegan Paul, Boston, MA.

Goodman, K. and Goodman, Y.M. (1977) Learning about psycholinguistic processes by analyzing oral reading, *Harvard Educational Review*, Vol. 47, no. 3, pp. 317–33.

Goodman, Y. and Burke, C. (1972) *Reading Miscue Inventory*, Macmillan, New York.

Goswami, U. (1994) Phonological skills, analogies and reading development, *Reading*, Vol. 28, no. 2, pp. 32–7.

Goswami, U. and Bryant, P. (1990) *Phonological Skills and Learning to Read*, Lawrence Erlbaum Associates, Hove.

Gray, N. (1994) *A Balloon for Grandad*, Orchard, London.

Gregory, E. (1995) What counts as reading in this class? Children's views, in P. Murphy, M. Selinger, J. Bourne and M. Briggs (eds) *Subject Learning in the Primary Curriculum*, Routledge, London.

Gregory, E. (1996) *Making Sense of a New World*, Paul Chapman Publishing, London.

Hall, N., Hemming, G., Hann, H. and Crawford, L. (1989) *Parental Views on Writing and the Teaching of Writing*, Department of Education Studies, Manchester Polytechnic, Manchester.

Halliday, M.A.K. (1975) *Learning how to Mean: Explorations in the Development of Language*, London, Edward Arnold.

Hallliday, M.A.K. and Hassan, R. (1985) *Language, Context and Text*, Oxford University Press, London.

Hancock, R. (1995) Hackney PACT, home reading programmes and family literacy, in B. Raban-Bisby, G. Brooks and S. Wolfendale (eds) *Developing Language and Literacy*, Trentham Books, Stoke-on-Trent.

Harrison, C. and Coles, M. (eds) (1992) *The Reading for Real Handbook*, Routledge, London.

Hertrich, J. (1997) HMI talks to NATE Council about OFSTED findings on English teaching, *NATE News*, Autumn, p. 5.

Hester, H. (1983) *Stories in the Multilingual Classroom*, Harcourt Brace Jovanovich, London.

Hewison, J. and Tizard, J. (1980) Parental involvement and reading attainment, *British Journal of Educational Psychology*, no. 50, part 3, pp. 209–15.

Hill, E. (1980) *Where's Spot?*, Heinemann, London.

Hills, T. (1986) *Classroom Motivation: Helping Students to Want to Learn and Achieve in School*, New Jersey Department of Education, Trenton, NJ.

HMI (1990) *The Teaching and Learning of Language and Literacy*, HMSO, London.

HMI (1991) *The Teaching and Learning of Reading in Primary Schools*, HMSO, London.

HMI (1993) *The HMI Report on the Implementation of the Curricular Requirements of the Education Reform Act English Key Stages 1, 2 and 3: Third Year, 1991–92*, HMSO, London.

HMI (1996) *The Teaching of Reading in 45 Inner London Primary Schools*, OFSTED Publications, London.

Hodgeon, J. (1984) *A Woman's World?*, Cleveland Education Authority and the Equal Opportunities Commission, Manchester.

Holdaway, D. (1979) *The Foundations of Literacy*, Ashton Scholastic, Sydney, NSW.

Hughes, S. (1996) *Enchantment in the Garden*, The Bodley Head, London.

Hunter-Grundin, E. (1997) Are reading standards falling?, *English in Education*, Vol. 31, no. 3, pp. 40–4.

Hutchins, P. (1968) *Rosie's Walk*, The Bodley Head, London.

Jackson, A. and Hannon, P. (1981) *The Belfield Reading Project*, Belfield Community Council, Rochdale.

Lazim, A. and Moss, E. (1997) *The Core Booklist*, CLPE, London.

Lewis, M.M. (1953) *The Importance of Illiteracy*, Harrap, London.

Littlefair, A.B. (1991) *Reading All Types of Writing*, Open University Press, Milton Keynes.

Lobban, G. (1975) Sex-roles in reading schemes, *Educational Review*, Vol. 27, no. 3, pp. 202–28.

Lochrie, M., Mansfield, M. and Pugh, G. (1993) *Parents and Early Learning, Report to the RSA Early Learning Project*, Royal Society of Arts, London.

Mallet, M. (1992) *Making Facts Matter: Reading Non-Fiction 5–11*, Paul Chapman Publishing, London.

Maris, R. (1985) *My Book*, Puffin Books, Harmondsworth.

McCracken, R.A. (1971) Initiating sustained silent reading, *Journal of Reading*, Vol. 14, no. 8, pp. 521–83.

McKee, D. (1980) *Not Now Bernard*, Andersen Press, London.

McNally, J. and Murray, W. (1968) *Key Words to Literacy* (2nd edn), Schoolmaster Publishing Company, London.

Medwell, J. (1996) Read well!, *Language and Literacy News*, no. 19.

Meek, M. (1988) *How Texts Teach What Readers Learn*, Thimble Press, Stroud.

Meek, M. (1993) What will literacy be like?, *Cambridge Journal of Education*, Vol. 23, no. 1, pp. 89–100.

Merchant, G. (1992) Supporting readers for whom English is a second language, in C. Harrison and M. Coles (eds) *The Reading for Real Handbook*, Routledge, London.

Minns, H. (1990) *Read It To Me Now!*, Virago, London.

Mound, L. (1993) *Amazing Insects*, Dorling Kindersley, London.

Murphy, J. (1982) *On the Way Home*, Picturemac, London.

NCC (1993) *National Curriculum Council Consultation Report: English in the National Curriculum*, NCC, York.

Neate, B. (1992) *Finding Out About Finding Out: A Practical Guide to Children's Information Books*, Hodder & Stoughton, London.

Nutbrown, C. (1997) *Recognising Early Literacy Development: Assessing Children's Achievements*, Paul Chapman Publishing, London.

OFSTED (1993) *Handbook for the Inspection of Schools*, HMSO, London.

O'Neil, W. (1977) Properly literate, in M. Hoyle (ed) *The Politics of Literacy*, Writers & Readers, London.

QCA (1997) *Can Do Better: Raising Boys' Achievement in English*, QCA, London.

Redfern, A. (1996) *Practical Ways to Teach Phonics*, Reading and Language Information Centre, The University of Reading.

Ridley, A. (1995) 'It's not the same as the real world': boys, girls, books and gender, in Bearne, E. (ed) *Greater Expectations*, Cassell, London.

Ross, T. (1991) *A Fairy Tale*, Andersen Press, London.

Sainsbury, M. (1996) *Tracking Significant Achievement in Primary English*, Hodder & Stoughton, London.

SCAA (1995a) *Planning the Curriculum at Key Stages 1 and 2*, SCAA, London.

SCAA (1995b) *Consistency in Teacher Assessment Exemplification of Standards*, SCAA, London.

SCAA (1996a) *Desirable Outcomes for Children's Learning*, HMSO, London.

SCAA (1996b) *Boys and English*, SCAA, London.

SCAA (1996c) *Standardised Literacy Tests in Primary Schools: Their Use and Usefulness*, SCAA, London.

SCAA (1997a) *Baseline Assessment Scales*, SCAA, London.

SCAA (1997b) *The National Framework for Baseline Assessment*, SCAA, London.

Schermbrucker, R. (1992) *Charlie's House*, Walker, London.

Schonell, F.J. (1945) *The Psychology and Teaching of Reading*, Oliver & Boyd, London.

Skelton, C. (1997) Revisiting gender issues in reading schemes, *Education 3 to 13*, Vol. 25, no. 1, pp. 37–43.

Smith, J. and Alcock, A. (1990) *Revisiting Literacy*, Open University Press, Milton Keynes.

Smith, L. (1995) *Dat's New Year*, A. & C. Black, London.

Snow, A. (1995) *The Truth about Cats*, HarperCollins, London.

Stacey, M. (1991) *Parents and Teachers Together*, Open University Press, Milton Keynes.

Stannard, J. (1995) National Literacy Project, *Child Education*, March, pp. 10–11.

Stanovich, K. (1980) Towards an interactive-compensatory model of individual reading differences in the development of reading fluency, *Reading Research Quarterly*, Vol. 16, no. 1, pp. 32–71.

Sylva, K. (1997) The early years curriculum: evidence-based proposals, paper presented to SCAA, 10 June.

Sylvester, R. (1991) *Start with a Story*, Development Education Centre, Birmingham.

Topping, K.J. and Lindsay, G. (1992) Paired reading: a review of the literature, *Research Papers in Education*, Vol. 7, no. 3, pp. 199–246.

Topping, K. and Wolfendale, S. (1985) *Parental Involvement in Children's Reading*, Croom Helm, London.

TTA (1997) *Teaching: High Status, High Standards (Circular No 10/97)*, DfEE, London.

UNESCO (1988) *1990: International Literacy Year (ILY) (ED/ILY/88.10)*, UNESCO, Paris.

Verma, G.K. (1984) *Papers on Biliteracy and Bilingualism*, National Council for Mother Tongue Teaching, London.

Waddell, M. (1994) *When the Teddy Bears Came*, Walker, London.

Wade, B. (1990) *Reading for Real*, Open University Press, Milton Keynes.

Wade, B. and Moore, M. (1987) *Special Children . . . Special Needs*, Robert Royce, London.

Wantanabe, S. (1977) *How Do I Put It On?*, Puffin Books, Harmondsworth.

Webster, A., Beveridge, M. and Reed, M. (1996) *Managing the Literacy Curriculum*, Routledge, London.

Weinberger, J. (1996) *Literacy Goes to School*, Paul Chapman Publishing, London.

Whitehead, M. (1996) *The Development of Language and Literacy*, Hodder & Stoughton, London.

Williams, V.A. (1993) *Dave and the Tooth Fairy*, Tamarind, Camberley.

Zimet, S.G. (1976) *Print and Prejudice*, Hodder & Stoughton, London.

# Index